The Effects of Praise

by
Andrew Wommack

HOW is true praise birth

ALBURY PUBLISHING
Tulsa, Oklahoma

The Effects of Praise
ISBN 1-57778-088-4
Copyright © 1998 by Andrew Wommack
P. O. Box 3333
Colorado Springs, Colorado 80934

Published by ALBURY PUBLISHING
P. O. Box 470406
Tulsa, Oklahoma 74147-0406

Contents

Contents

Preface

Praise affects every area of our life — our personal relationship with God, our spiritual warfare against the devil, and our own mental and emotional well-being. Praise is something a Christian just cannot do without. It ought to be the first thing we do each morning to begin our day, and it ought to be the last thing we do each evening to end our day. We should begin and end every prayer with praise unto the Lord. The Scripture admonishes us to constantly praise the Lord — in the morning, at noon, and when the sun goes down.

God desires to have a relationship with every believer, and we develop that relationship through studying His Word and spending time communing with Him. Praise is a part of that. Praise brings intimacy, and when we experience an intimate relationship with the Father, we experience eternal life.

I really believe that our ministry unto the Lord through praise is the most important thing we can do in our Christian walk. If we would begin to operate in this and understand how praise affects the Lord and how it ministers unto Him, this would provide the basis of a foundation that will last us through our life — not only in crisis times, but throughout the entire time we're here on the earth.

There is so much material on the subject of praise. The purpose of this book is to emphasize and to help us understand why praise is so important. There are three areas, I believe, that have much more revelation from God's Word about what praise accomplishes than what most Christians have seen — the effect praise has on the believer, the effect praise has on the devil, and the effect praise has on God.

This book will show you how you can walk in a new level of praise in your personal relationship with the Lord. You will be amazed at the effect a praise-filled life will have on your daily life and on your relationship with God.

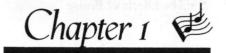

Chapter 1

Why We Praise

Praise is much more important than what the average person thinks. A lot of Christians believe it is nice to praise God and to be thankful unto Him, but they really look at it as being something that's optional. In other words, it would be good if we praised God, but if we don't it's certainly understandable and no one would look at it as being sin.

Yet, that is not the picture painted in the Word of God. It is a direct *command* of God. It is not an *option*. Praise is a necessity, as we see in Deuteronomy.

> Moreover all these curses shall come upon thee, and shall pursue thee, and overtake thee, till thou be destroyed; because thou hearkenedst not unto the voice of the Lord thy God, to keep his commandments and his statutes which he commanded thee:
>
> And they shall be upon thee for a sign and for a wonder, and upon thy seed for ever.
>
> Because thou servedst not the Lord thy God with joyfulness, and with gladness of heart, for the abundance of all things;
>
> Therefore shalt thou serve thine enemies which the Lord shall send against thee, in

hunger, and in thirst, and in nakedness, and in want of all things: and he shall put a yoke of iron upon thy neck, until he have destroyed thee.
Deuteronomy 28:45-48

Even though this is not written directly to us, as we are not the children of Israel and are not under this covenant, it is still written for our admonition and learning. We see how seriously God looks at praise from His people. The reason God was bringing all these curses upon them was because they didn't serve the **Lord thy God with joyfulness, and with gladness of heart, for the abundance of all things.** That was sin in God's eyes!

When we think of God's judgment coming upon the Israelites in the Old Testament, we think of gross sins such as idolatry, immorality, murder, etc. But very few people think about God bringing judgment upon people because they didn't have joy and they weren't thankful for what He had done. Their immorality was also a part of their judgment, but a lack of joy and gladness of heart was included in their sin. They were not thankful for the abundance of things God had given them. Praise was not being returned unto God.

That takes praise out of the category of being optional — something that would be nice to do if we wanted to, if we felt like it, or if it was convenient. This elevates it to a realm that God intended it to be.

He Is Worthy of Our Praise

If you have nothing to praise God for, if there is nothing good in your life, you are still to praise God. Why? Because He is worthy!

The writer of Psalm 107 begins by saying, **O give thanks unto the Lord, for he is good: for his mercy endureth for ever.** Then for the next six verses, he gives praise unto God for all the great works He had done for the nation of Israel — specifically that He brought them out of the land of Egypt, that He performed all the miracles, and that He delivered them from their distress. Throughout this psalm, he recounted these words four different times, **Oh that men would praise the Lord for his goodness, and for his wonderful works to the children of men!**

He isn't saying that men should praise the Lord because it will benefit them personally, although it will. He isn't saying to praise the Lord because it will overcome our enemy, although that is truth. He was speaking from God's perspective. He was relating the heart of God and telling the people to give praise unto God for His goodness. In other words, God is worthy to be praised.

God deserves our praise. He has done so much for us, yet many times we fail to recognize that He desires our praise in return. God longs for that. It's very similar to a parent-child relationship. God loves us as a parent loves a child, and He wants our love in return. So in this sense, God has a need and God needs that love returned.

Imagine if you really loved someone and showered your love upon them. I mean, you loved them so much, even to the point that you took your own son and sacrificed him so this other person might go free. Now if you did all of that for them and they turned around and didn't thank you for it, would that please you? If they weren't thankful, if they didn't minister back unto you, would you be blessed? It's inconceivable that a person who really loves and shows that love wouldn't want to be loved in return. Any person who loves has a need to also be loved.

I believe God has that need. Don't misunderstand me — I'm not saying that God is depressed, discouraged, or He's bummed out because He's not receiving the love that is due unto Him. God is greater than that. But I do believe that God desires our love, and I believe He is not pleased when we are not loving Him the way we should. I'm not saying He dislikes us, but it displeases Him because He desires our praise.

Give unto the Lord the glory due unto his name; worship the Lord in the beauty of holiness.

Psalm 29:2

All the earth shall worship thee, and shall sing unto thee; they shall sing to thy name. Selah.

Psalm 66:4

I will praise the Lord according to his righteousness: and will sing praise to the name of the Lord most high.

Psalm 7:17

Whoso offereth praise glorifieth me.

Psalm 50:23

I will bless the Lord at all times: his praise shall continually be in my mouth.

Psalm 34:1

Bless the Lord, O my soul: and all that is within me, bless his holy name.

Psalm 103:1

We are instructed throughout Scripture to praise the Lord, to give Him glory, and to worship Him.

I like Psalm 100:4,

Enter into his gates with thanksgiving, and into his courts with praise: be thankful unto him, and bless his name.

That is the way our relationship with Him should be. That is how we should begin our prayer — by entering His gates with thanksgiving and His courts with praise. This is how God desires it to be, because He loves us and wants to receive that love in return.

I was at a missions conference one time, and a man was talking about the importance of missions. He made the statement that the sole justification for our existence on the earth is to lead another person to the Lord. I understood the point he was trying to make. He was trying to encourage people to recognize, "Hey, we are supposed to be out sharing our faith."

I agreed with his heart and with the point he was making, but when he said that, the Lord spoke to me and said, "No, no, no, that is not the sole justification. That is not the only way you can justify your existence here on this earth."

This is something I feel most Christians have misunderstood. We think that our net worth to God — the only thing we really have to offer Him — is just our service. That's not true. God longs for us personally, not just what we can give Him, not just what we can do for Him. He wants our affection, that we desire and love and worship Him.

Praise Brings Pleasure to God

Our number one priority has to be to love God personally — not just love Him through the things we do for Him or what He can do for us, but to *love God*. It's not enough to just give God our tithes, we need to give God our heart. If God gets our heart, He'll get our pocketbook, He'll get our service, He'll get everything else there is to have. God wants *us*, not just what we can do for Him.

Look at Adam and Eve as an example. Revelation 4:11 says, **for thy pleasure they are and were created.** The original purpose Adam was created for is still the same purpose God has for people today — for His pleasure. What was the justification for Adam and Eve's existence? Before sin entered into the earth, how could they justify their existence? Adam and Eve didn't have a church to work in and to serve. They didn't have anyone to minister to or cast devils out of. There were no sick to lay hands on and see recover. There was no one who needed them to pray for prosperity. So what was the justification for Adam and Eve's existence?

I believe that you'd have to say it was for the Lord's pleasure. God created them to be an object of His love so He could love them and minister to them, but also so they would be there to love Him back. It was a two-way street — a two-way communication. God got pleasure out of fellowshipping with Adam and Eve on a daily basis. That was His purpose in creating man. God created man because He wanted someone to fellowship with, to commune with, and to have pleasure in.

Praise Is God's Will for Us

Thou art worthy, O Lord, to receive glory and honour and power: for thou hast created all things, and for thy pleasure they are and were created.

Revelation 4:11

This scripture is what the twenty-four elders around the throne room in heaven cry out to God. This shows that God's original purpose for creation is for His pleasure. That purpose has not changed. He created us to give Him pleasure and this pleasure refers to praise and worship. If this is the way it is in heaven, then this is the way God intends for it to be here on earth.

Jesus prayed in Matthew 6:10, **Thy will be done in earth, as it is in heaven.** In heaven, there is constant praise. That is God's will for us. God created us to be full of praise, full of joy, and full of thanksgiving. We were created to be worshippers of God. That is not just for a few people, but for every born-again person.

Satan tries to thwart this. He tried to stop all of heaven from worshipping God, and now he's trying to stop us from worshipping God on an individual level. But worship is reserved for God alone.

Peace Is a Benefit of Praise

Rejoice in the Lord alway: and again I say, Rejoice.
Let your moderation be known unto all men. The Lord is at hand.
Be careful for nothing; but in every thing by prayer and supplication with thanksgiving let your requests be made known unto God.
And the peace of God, which passeth all understanding, shall keep your hearts and minds through Christ Jesus.
Philippians 4:4-7

When we let our requests be made known with thanksgiving, then the **peace... which passeth all understanding, shall keep your hearts and minds through Christ Jesus.** It's only when we pray with thanksgiving that the peace of God will keep our heart and mind. Peace is not a product of circumstances. Peace doesn't come when there are no problems. That's the way the world looks at it. But peace — God's kind of peace — is something that is there even in the midst of problems. It is a result of keeping our minds stayed on God. I've been in situations where, in the natural, there was no reason that I should have joy or peace. But because I had my mind focused on God and His promises, because I had faith working on the inside of me, I had peace. And it's exactly like these scriptures say, that when you **let your requests be made known unto God... the peace of God, which passeth all understanding, shall keep your hearts and minds through Christ Jesus.** When you are praising God, a super-natural peace will follow, a peace that no man can understand or explain. There is no physical reason for it, but the peace of God *will* keep your heart and mind.

> **Thou wilt keep him in perfect peace, whose mind is stayed on thee: because he trusteth in thee.**

> **Isaiah 26:3**

If your mind is stayed on God, you will have perfect peace. If your mind is not stayed on God, you will not have perfect peace. If you aren't experiencing peace in your life, most likely your mind is not stayed on God. (See Romans 8:6.)

Some people will argue with me and say, "But wait a minute. You don't understand my problem. You don't know my situation. How can I have peace?" They have just shown me their problem. Their attention is focused on their problem and not on the answer. Their attention is focused only on the natural realm. But there is another world out there. Even if every time they see light at the end of the tunnel it turns out to be another train, they still don't have to be in turmoil, because if worse came to worse, what could happen? They would die and go to be with the Lord! That's the peace that passes all understanding.

Praise Is Strength

> **Out of the mouth of babes and sucklings hast thou ordained strength because of thine enemies, that thou mightest still the enemy and the avenger.**

> **Psalm 8:2**

When Jesus made His triumphal entry into the city of Jerusalem on what we call Palm Sunday, thousands of people turned out to greet him, singing, **Hosanna to the son of David** (Matthew 21:15). This greatly upset the Pharisees and the chief priests because they considered this blasphemy.

And it would have been blasphemy if Jesus was not God. But Jesus was God, therefore it was appropriate for the people to worship Him.

The religious people expected Jesus to rebuke the multitude for such an outcry, but instead, Jesus quoted Psalm 8:2, except He changed one phrase. In verse 16 of Matthew 21, we find that Jesus replied, **Out of the mouth of babes and sucklings thou hast perfected praise.** By comparing these two scriptures, we see that Jesus interchanged the phrase *perfected praise* for *ordained strength*. Praise is strength! If you think praise is optional, you won't see it that way. But Nehemiah says the same thing in Nehemiah 8:10, **The joy of the Lord is your strength.**

This strength is specifically to be used against our enemy. It says that it stops the enemy and the avenger. Praise is the greatest weapon we have against Satan and his daily onslaught. It literally makes Satan flee in terror when we begin to praise God, and the anointing of God is able to manifest itself in the absence of opposition from the devil. Praise *is* spiritual warfare.

I have seen many people get into what they call spiritual warfare, but it is actually depressing. They are fighting the devil and spending more time with the devil than they are with God. That's not right. Yes, there is a place for fighting and resisting the devil, but maintaining an attitude of praise is the best weapon we have.

If sickness tries to come upon your body, instead of spending so much time dealing with the devil and making that your priority, begin to praise God and thank Him for the healing that has been promised to you. The medical profession has statistics that show that a happy and joyful person is much more healthy than a person who is morbid, sad, and depressed. Praise God for healing you, and let the joy of the Lord be your strength.

Praise Blesses the Lord

So many people were seeking Him that sometimes Jesus would have to stay up all night praying and fellowshipping with the Father because He couldn't do it during the daylight hours. Jesus gave priority to a personal relationship with God, and it's got to be the same for every individual member in the Body of Christ. We must recognize that this is what makes everything else function. If our personal relationship with God is sagging, then everything else will eventually crumble. The way we establish this personal relationship with the Lord is not limited to praise, but I believe that praise is the way to begin this love relationship with God.

If we begin to bless the Lord, tell Him how much we love Him, and thank Him for what He's done, I guarantee you God will minister His love back to us.

An example of this happened about ten years ago when I took my two boys, Joshua and Peter, out to ride our horses. I also bought them junk food — ice cream and all kinds of things. We just spent the whole day riding horses, playing in the creek, wrestling, and having a great time. When they were going to bed that night, I kissed Peter goodnight, turned off the light, and as I walked out of the room, Peter said, "Dad?"

I said, "Yep."

"You're a good dad." And do you know, what he said blessed me. Boy, I mean it made my heart jump up and down and do flip-flops!

He was saying "thank-you" in his own way. Now he didn't say, "Bless you, Dad." No, what he said was, "Dad, you're a good dad," and his saying that blessed me. When the Scripture admonishes us to bless the Lord, that's what it's talking about. God gets blessed by us expressing our love and worship and praise unto Him.

A good friend of mine had a revelation of how much God loves him. He was in a terrible situation in a mental ward, got a revelation of God's love for him, and got born again. As a result, he's now a tremendous man of God — pastors a church and sees great things happen. But he has a saying that he says to a lot of people, "God loves me. God carries my picture in His wallet." And then he tells other people, "God has my picture on His mantel."

There are some people who get offended at that. They think, "Man, who do you think you are? You think you're somebody special that you could bless God, that you have something you could offer to God?" But the point he's making is that God loves him. He got a revelation of that. He knows that when he loves God back and tells God he loves Him, that blesses God.

If you don't have a real revelation of God's love for you, or even if you do but you want more, just begin setting aside a special time each day to praise Him. I guarantee you'll enter into a deeper level of intimacy with Him and the rest of your day will go a whole lot better!

Chapter 2

How Could Paul Praise?

If we take a serious look at Paul's life, some of the apostles' lives, and even some of this country's early ministers and missionaries, it's easy to wonder how they could possibly continue to offer praise and worship to God in the midst of their sufferings. However, if we look further, we see how Paul viewed all of the suffering he went through.

> We are troubled on every side, yet not distressed; we are perplexed, but not in despair;
>
> Persecuted, but not forsaken; cast down, but not destroyed;
>
> Always bearing about in the body the dying of the Lord Jesus, that the life also of Jesus might be made manifest in our body.
>
> 2 Corinthians 4:8-10
>
> For our light affliction, which is but for a moment, worketh for us a far more exceeding and eternal weight of glory;
>
> While we look not at the things which are seen, but at the things which are not seen: for the things which are seen are temporal; but the things which are not seen are eternal.
>
> 2 Corinthians 4:17,18

Notice Paul said, **our light affliction.** This is an amazing statement! Sometimes we skip over this and don't really understand the background of what Paul was saying. If we look in chapter 11 of 2 Corinthians, Paul mentions what his light afflictions were.

> **For ye suffer, if a man bring you into bondage, if a man devour you, if a man take of you, if a man exalt himself, if a man smite you on the face.**
>
> **Are they ministers of Christ? (I speak as a fool) I am more; in labours more abundant, in stripes above measure, in prisons more frequent, in deaths oft.**
>
> **Of the Jews five times received I forty stripes save one.**
>
> **Thrice was I beaten with rods, once was I stoned, thrice I suffered shipwreck, a night and a day I have been in the deep;**
>
> **In journeyings often, in perils of waters, in perils of robbers, in perils by mine own countrymen, in perils by the heathen, in perils in the city, in perils in the wilderness, in perils in the sea, in perils among false brethren;**
>
> **In weariness and painfulness, in watchings often, in hunger and thirst, in fastings often, in cold and nakedness.**
>
> **2 Corinthians 11:20,23-27**

Paul had been through the wringer! He even said that he had suffered more than anyone, yet he considered it a "light affliction." He wasn't saying it was a light affliction because he didn't have as many problems as you and I do. Paul probably suffered more than you and I have ever thought about suffering, but it was just a light affliction for him because of his perspective.

I hear so many people say, "I would praise God if I didn't have so many problems." And then they begin enumerating all of their problems. In effect, they're saying, "Yes, I agree with praise, and I would praise God if it were easier, but it's just too hard with all the problems I'm facing." Paul had it worse than anyone, yet he said it was just a light affliction and praised God in the midst of everything. Now if Paul, who had more problems and more adversity than any of us, could praise God, then *no one* is justified in not praising God because of their problems.

The Choice Is Ours

Satan has deceived the Body of Christ. He has built elaborate systems of justifying people's lack of praise.

Psychology has also had a big impact on our society today — and not all of it is good. Primarily, it has taken blame and responsibility away from us. We aren't responsible for our actions. It's another person's fault. It's our parents and the way they did or didn't treat us. It's society, the color of our skin, if we had more money, if we had this or that. We blame our sin or bad habits on everyone and everything else. Yet Paul, who had terrible adversity come against him, never blamed anyone else. He took responsibility for his emotions and he chose to praise God.

Given our present-day situations, we have the choice of how we are going to respond. Society can't *make* us respond a particular way. Our circumstances can't *make* us have behavioral problems. It's our choice. When God created us, He gave us the ability to choose. Just as we have the ability to choose eternal life or death, we have the ability to choose to praise God in all situations.

Deuteronomy 30:19 says,

**I call heaven and earth to record this day
against you, that I have set before you life and
death, blessing and cursing: therefore choose
life, that both thou and thy seed may live.**

God gave *us* the choice. He doesn't make the choice for us,
and Satan cannot force us into any decision. It's *our* choice.

The choice isn't difficult. It's either life or death, blessing
or cursing. This should be a "no-brainer." But just in case
someone might be having trouble with the choice, God gives
us a hint. He says, "Choose life." It's like a test with the
choices (a) life or (b) death. And then God puts in parentheses that (a) is the answer.

My dad died when I was only twelve years old. I went
through the teenage years, the most critical time of my life,
without a father. Psychologists would gladly tell you all of the
problems I should have. My dad was always sick. He would
come home from work and need to rest. He didn't go on
camping trips. He never threw a baseball with me. We never
played football. We never did any of the things that kids are
supposed to do with their father, and I still loved him dearly.
I had a good relationship with him and have nothing but good
memories of him. When he died I missed him, but I understood that he wasn't there. I wasn't bitter toward him.

I've met women who have lost their husbands either
through divorce or through death, and they are just panic-
stricken about their children — "They have to have a father!"
They are willing to marry the first guy who walks down the
street just so their children will have a father.

That's an example of this mentality that says, "We just
can't prosper if we're in this adversity. The only way we're
really going to succeed is if we can change our situation and
get to the place where we have no more problems." But that's
not true. I grew up in a situation that most people would have
said was desperate, but I can honestly say that I can't see a

single problem I had growing up through those teenage years without my father that I couldn't overcome.

Some people do become bitter and resentful toward a parent who is no longer with them. Not every teenager has fond memories of that missing parent. Some kids have a two-parent home, but the father is so involved in his business that he is never home to participate in that child's life. But we have a choice to make. We can choose to respond in light of God's Word and be better, or we can choose to respond according to our flesh and be bitter. We can either be better or bitter. It's our choice.

Paul's Ultimate Desire

For I am in a strait betwixt two, having a desire to depart, and to be with Christ; which is far better:

Nevertheless to abide in the flesh is more needful for you.

Philippians 1:23,24

Paul recognized the benefit of going to be with the Lord. That was his ultimate desire. But he also knew there was more work for him to do on this earth to further the Gospel. And so hesitantly or regretfully he says, "I guess I'll stay here with you so that I can benefit you." That's a man whose perspective was right. That's a man who operated in praise.

So what about our situation today? If we are struggling in the area of healing, we need to get our mind off of our negative circumstances and begin to praise God and think about God's healing. Even if we don't receive a manifestation of healing in this life, the worst that could happen is that we would die and go to be with the Lord. He has so much laid up for us that we should have the attitude Paul did, where we can say, "I have a desire to depart and to be with the Lord."

> **I want to know Christ and the power of his resurrection and the fellowship of sharing in his sufferings.**
>
> **Philippians 3:10 NIV**

Paul understood that when he was being persecuted it wasn't really him being persecuted, it was Jesus. Jesus told Paul that. When he was converted on the road to Damascus, the Lord appeared to him and said, "Saul, why are you persecuting Me?" (See Acts 9:3-5.) Saul had not physically persecuted Jesus, but he was persecuting the followers of Jesus, and Jesus put it into first person and said, "You are persecuting Me."

I believe Paul thought on those things. He remembered his conversion experience and realized it wasn't him being persecuted, it was Jesus. Jesus was suffering through Paul, and he began to praise God. It was a decision of his will based upon the things he was thinking about. If he would have thought about his problem, his pain, and his discomfort; if he would have thought about how unjust the Romans were and what they were doing to him, he would have been discouraged. But instead he chose to operate in praise.

Overcoming a Pressure Cooker

Paul chose to respond to his pressures in a positive way. We cannot justify being negative, depressed, or discouraged by our circumstances. I admit, these responses are a temptation — they are a pressure. But ultimately we make the choice. If the pressure on the inside of us is greater than the pressure that is on the outside of us, we won't crumble, regardless of what happens.

Praise is one of those things that builds up spiritual pressure on the inside. Praise puts our attention on God and releases the strength of the Lord on the inside of us. If the joy of the Lord is our strength, when we operate in praise and choose to glorify God, strength will flow in us.

I remember a science experiment my class did when I was in the sixth grade. We took a one-gallon metal gas can, put it on a burner, and heated it until the can got very hot. Now when air gets hot it expands. So the air expanded inside that gas can and while it was still hot, we immediately put the cap on it to make it airtight. We then let the can cool down. As it cooled, the air inside the can began to compress and a partial vacuum formed. Then we watched the can just crumple. The atmospheric pressure of our classroom crushed the can because the pressure outside was greater than the pressure inside.

That experiment made a big impression on me. It illustrated what I'm saying about having a spiritual pressure built up inside of us so it is stronger than the outside pressures of life we face everyday. Praise builds that spiritual pressure! Praise releases the strength of the Lord inside of us.

Everyone experiences pressure. Paul went through more pressures than what any of us claim to go through, yet he says, "It's just a light affliction." He didn't say this because he didn't have any problems or outside pressures trying to crumple him, but the pressure he had on the inside was greater. Paul had the right perspective, and that's what praise will do for us.

Praise will keep us built up on the inside. It will keep our mind stayed on God. The Lord will keep us in perfect peace. It doesn't matter what pressures are coming against us, praise can keep us from crumpling and from being crushed under those pressures.

Paul's Two Weapons

There were two main things Paul was aware of that kept him built up with more pressure on the inside than there was on the outside. First, he said, "This light affliction is just for a moment." Now when he said "just for a moment," he didn't mean just sixty seconds! No, he was looking at it in light of *eternity*.

Paul had pressures come against him throughout his entire ministry. In 2 Corinthians 12:7, he talked about a messenger of Satan that plagued him everywhere he went — it was persecution. Paul was persecuted everywhere he went. This wasn't something that just happened for one minute. It happened throughout his lifetime. And the Lord said that he wouldn't remove this persecution from him, but that His grace was sufficient for him. (See 2 Corinthians 12:9.)

In other words, God says, "You can bear up under it. The pressure on the inside of you is great enough that you can take any of the pressure Satan brings to bear on you." Paul saw his life as just a moment compared to eternity and all of the time he had yet to spend with God.

If the pressures in your life seem too big, one of the reasons is because you're looking at them only in the light of your immediate situation. You need to kick back and remember, "This is just temporary. It will pass. God's grace is sufficient to see me through this situation."

One of my favorite scripture phrases is, "It came to pass." That's why it came — so it could pass! All our problems are only temporary.

Everything that comes against us is only for a moment or a season. Even though Paul was persecuted, plagued, and buffeted everywhere he went, compared to eternity, it was just a brief period of time. We need to remind ourselves of this.

If you're unequally yoked with someone, the situation has become oppressive, and you listen to mankind, they'll say, "You've been at this for a whole year! How long are you going to stand?" They'll make it sound like you're just stupid for standing on the Word and believing God's promises. But when you look at it in the light of eternity, you stand for

twenty, thirty, or forty years and it's but for a moment —
nothing compared to eternity.

You see, this life on earth is not all there is. There will be
a time when we will stand before God, look back at what
we've done in this life, and wish we would have thought about
eternity and how brief this life was. Make this life count for
the most that it possibly can!

The second thing that Paul had going for him was that he
saw his circumstances and problems as a "light affliction."
Praise puts everything in its proper perspective.

Looking at our situation as a light affliction and something
that will last just for a moment will change our attitudes. Now
I believe in healing, but sometimes people struggle with their
healing when it doesn't seem to come as soon as it should.
They think, "Am I ever going to get healed?" But if worse
comes to worse, praise God, we'll be totally healed in eternity!

That attitude should take the pressure off of you. It will
stop your complaints. It will take away the negative thoughts
and fears. It will enable your faith to grow. Paul said in
Philippians 1:21 that **to live is Christ, and to die is gain.**
There are no diseases, no financial troubles, and no marriage
or family problems in heaven. They're all wiped away. Praising
God for the promises He's made unto us is superpowerful!

Seeing the Spiritual Realm

**While we look not at the things which are
seen, but at the things which are not seen: for
the things which are seen are temporal; but
the things which are not seen are eternal.**

2 Corinthians 4:18

Another reason Paul was able to call his problems a light
affliction was because he was looking into the spiritual realm.
He was seeing what God was doing. He was operating in

faith. And the truth is that every time we encounter something negative, every time we see the devil doing something, I promise you that God is also at work! God has a *plan* and a *purpose* for your life. (See Jeremiah 29:11.) Trust Him, believe His Word, and watch His destiny for your life come to pass.

If we exert our faith and look into the spiritual realm of things, those spiritual things will dominate us instead of the physical things we see around us. Paul operated in this. He didn't look just at things that could be seen. He looked at things that could not be seen. He looked at the promises of God. Now there are many ways we can do that, but one of those ways is through praise.

Praise focuses our attention on the promises of God. Praise puts our attention on the things that are not seen. If we are in a tight situation, we have to get beyond what we can see and look at the unseen. Praise will do that. Praise will push us into a realm of seeing what God has done for us.

In Acts 16:22, Paul and Silas were thrown into prison at midnight for preaching the Gospel. They were thrown into a dark, damp, rat-infested, disease-ridden dungeon — the lowest part of the prison. Their hands and feet were put in stocks. And I guarantee you, they didn't have any laws governing the treatment of prisoners. It was a bad situation. I doubt that this was the most encouraging moment of their day! They didn't feel joy coming upon them.

But Paul and Silas weren't looking at the things that were seen — they were looking at the things that were not seen. They were looking at the Answer. They began to praise and worship God, not knowing exactly how God would deliver them, but they praised Him — their Answer.

In the midst of that prison cell, Paul and Silas began to praise and worship God, and when they did, an earthquake came. This was no coincidence. This earthquake was directly from God, and the praise of God is what released it. Praise released delivering power and they were set free from that negative situation.

What Does It All Mean for Us?

There are many Christians today fighting depression and discouragement. As I travel around and minister, I've seen as many as 80 to 90 percent of the Spirit-filled Christians in church stand up when I give an invitation for people who are discouraged. Now I'm not condemning people, but it is wrong for Spirit-filled Christians to be constantly fighting depression and discouragement.

I can hear you say, "But you don't understand my circumstances." You're right, I don't understand your circumstances. But your circumstances aren't worse than what Paul's circumstances were in 2 Corinthians 4, and he was able to rejoice and say, "They're just a light affliction." It is not your circumstances that are making you depressed. It's the way you are responding to them. If you would choose to praise God, you could come out of those things. You could prosper. It doesn't matter what your circumstances are.

It is necessary for Christians to go beyond their physical circumstances. We need to get our mind off of the problem and begin to see the answer! Yes, we have problems. Yes, the enemy will come against us. But our trials are a "light affliction" and "but for a moment." We have eternity to look forward to!

Chapter 3 ♪

Praise in the Old Testament

Some people may say, "Well, I can see the benefits of praise, and it would be wonderful to keep my mind stayed on God. But you just don't understand my situation. It doesn't work that way for everyone." On the contrary, Paul wasn't the only person in the Bible to suffer. There are many examples in Scripture of men and women of God finding themselves in desperate situations.

Habakkuk

The Old Testament prophet Habakkuk wrote a very sad book in the sense that he pronounced judgment on the nation of Judah. The people had rejected God and had not obeyed His commands. Judah had been warned that their sinful ways were displeasing to God. They knew there needed to be repentance, yet they refused. So the dreaded Chaldeans came upon Judah and totally destroyed them. Then, at the very end of the book, this prophet who had pronounced nothing but gloom and doom came up with one of the most powerful statements on praise in the entire Word of God.

When I heard, my belly trembled; my lips quivered at the voice: rottenness entered into my

bones, and I trembled in myself, that I might rest in the day of trouble: when he cometh up unto the people, he will invade them with his troops.

Although the fig tree shall not blossom, neither shall fruit be in the vines; the labour of the olive shall fail, and the fields shall yield no meat; the flock shall be cut off from the fold, and there shall be no herd in the stalls:

Yet I will rejoice in the Lord, I will joy in the God of my salvation.

The Lord God is my strength, and he will make my feet like hinds' feet, and he will make me to walk upon mine high places.

Habakkuk 3:16-19

That's a tremendous statement! All of this gloom, all of this doom, all of this judgment, and he says, "Even though there's no food, even though the cattle are wasted, even though nothing is working for me, **yet I will rejoice in the Lord.**"

Rejoicing is a decision we make. It's something we choose to do. Many people have been lied to by the devil and by our society. There are attitudes in our society that we have accepted as being true without questioning them. One of those is: *If we feel bad, then we can't help it. We just have to be discouraged. We have to let those feelings dominate us.* That is not true. I'm sure Habakkuk did not feel goosebumps going up and down his spine as he began to praise God. But in the midst of this depressing situation, he chose to rejoice in the Lord and let the Lord God be his strength.

David

David found himself in a situation in 1 Samuel 30 where, for thirteen years, he had been anointed to be king. Because of his integrity, he had not taken the throne from Saul. He had plenty of opportunities to kill King Saul, who was living an ungodly life and was rejected by God, but David didn't do it. (See 1 Samuel 15:10-35.)

David operated in integrity and it cost him dearly. He lost his wife when Saul gave her to another man. (See 1 Samuel 18:19.) He was driven out of the nation of Israel. (See 1 Samuel 22:1-5.) On one occasion he acted like he was crazy, let spit run down his beard, and feigned being totally out of his mind to save his neck. (See 1 Samuel 21:13.) He was hungry. He was under pressure. He had nothing but the outcasts of Israel living with him and acting as his army. Finally, to top it all off, his wives, Abigail and Ahinoam, were captured by the Amalekites, who took all the women and children when they burned and plundered the city of Ziklag.

The way that affected David could have been traumatic. His own men, whom he had fed, defended, and taken care of, got angry and planned to stone him when they found their city plundered and their wives and children gone. (See 1 Samuel 30:1-6.)

In the midst of that situation, David wept before the Lord, and in 1 Samuel 30:6, it says he **was greatly distressed.** He was depressed. But it goes on to say that he **encouraged and strengthened himself in the Lord his God** (AMP). Instead of giving up, he did exactly what we are supposed to do. He was in the middle of terribly negative circumstances, but he focused his attention on God. He remembered the promises God had given him. He remembered the day Samuel had anointed him to be king. (See 1 Samuel 16:10-13.) He began to praise God with some of the very psalms that are written in the Bible, and in the midst of his circumstances, he encouraged himself in the Lord.

As a result, David was able to recapture all of the women and children who had been stolen by the Amalekites. He recovered all that they had lost, including his two wives. He even took all of the flocks and herds the Amalekites had gained. Most importantly, within just a number of days, he realized his vision of being king over Israel. If he had quit when he had been discouraged and depressed, he would have lost everything just forty-eight hours away from the fulfillment of his anointing. But you see, he encouraged himself in the Lord in the midst of a negative situation. And we can do that! We can encourage ourselves and gain strength from the Lord through praise.

The Scripture calls David **a man after** [God's] **own heart** (1 Samuel 13:14). I believe one of the things that made him a man after God's own heart was praise. He was constantly praising God. He didn't give in to depression. In 2 Samuel 6:16-23, it is recorded that he praised God so demonstratively in front of the entire nation of Israel, that his wife, Michal, called him a fool. As he was bringing the ark of the covenant back into the city of David, Michal looked out of her window, saw him dancing and praising God, and **despised him in her heart.** She was embarrassed because of his unbridled praise and worship unto God. Do you know what David's reaction was? He spoke of all the things God had done for him. He said he was nothing until the Lord called him and anointed him. Then he told her he would be even more demonstrative than this. He was willing to make a fool of himself in her eyes so he could glorify God.

Michal and David never did get over that problem. He had no more relationship with her until the day of her death, and she died a barren woman. But even when his wife made fun of him, he refused to give up his praise and worship unto God. That was his priority in life. That was what made him a man after God's own heart.

Elijah

It is so important that we keep our mind stayed on God. Elijah got his mind off the things of the Lord. He got to looking at the negative and got so depressed that he asked God to kill him. (See 1 Kings 19:4.) Finally, the Lord appeared to Elijah.

And the word of the Lord came to him: "What are you doing here, Elijah?"

He replied, "I have been very zealous for the Lord God Almighty. The Israelites have rejected your covenant, broken down your altars, and put your prophets to death with the sword. I am the only one left, and now they are trying to kill me too."

1 Kings 19:9,10 NIV

But that wasn't true. Elijah wasn't the only one left, and he knew it. Obadiah told him in verse 13 of the previous chapter that he had taken one hundred prophets and hidden them in two caves, with water and food supplies to last through the famine. There were others faithfully serving God. Elijah had an attitude! He had become negative, and that's all he could see — the negative side of things.

Our society today is a master at seeing the negative side of everything. We have glorified the negative. We report so many negative things that, sad to say, even the Church has become one of the greatest promoters of negativity. We love to talk about how bad the situation is. I think it actually makes us feel more justified when we aren't making the impact we should. We feel sorry for ourselves. "Oh, it's such a strong battle. I just can't help it." It takes some of the bite out of our failures.

God didn't kill Elijah like he asked. He had mercy on him and gave him Elisha, who ministered unto him. He also told Elijah in 1 Kings 19:18 that he was not alone. Seven thousand others were still serving God. Like Elijah, we need to get our eyes off of the negative and remember that God is still on the throne!

Jehoshaphat

In 2 Chronicles 20, we find Jehoshaphat, a godly king of Judah, in a real predicament. Three armies are about to come against him — the army of Moab, the army of Ammon, and the army of Mount Seir. These three armies joined together to come against the nation of Judah. When Jehoshaphat heard about it, he quickly called the entire nation together and proclaimed a fast. He stood before the people in the temple and prayed,

> O Lord God of our fathers, art not thou God in heaven? and rulest not thou over all the kingdoms of the heathen? and in thine hand is there not power and might, so that none is able to withstand thee?
>
> For we have no might against this great company that cometh against us; neither know we what to do: but our eyes are upon thee.
>
> 2 Chronicles 20:6,12

Then the people stood there and waited for God to do something. God sent them a prophet and the prophet gave them this word,

> Hearken ye, all Judah, and ye inhabitants of Jerusalem, and thou king Jehoshaphat, Thus saith the Lord unto you, Be not afraid nor dismayed by reason of this great multitude; for the battle is not yours, but God's.
>
> To morrow go ye down against them: behold, they come up by the cliff of Ziz; and ye

shall find them at the end of the brook, before
the wilderness of Jeruel.

Ye shall not need to fight in this battle: set
yourselves, stand ye still, and see the salvation
of the Lord with you, O Judah and Jerusalem:
fear not, nor be dismayed; to morrow go out
against them: for the Lord will be with you.

2 Chronicles 20:15-17

Jehoshaphat then bowed his face to the ground, along with
all of Judah and Jerusalem, and worshipped the Lord.
Immediately the Levites and the singers began praising God
with a loud voice. The word of deliverance came from the
Lord and immediately they began to praise God. *Our faith is
expressed through praise and worship.*

Jehoshaphat told them in verse 20, **Believe in the Lord
your God, so shall ye be established; believe his prophets,
so shall ye prosper.** He then consulted with the people and
came up with the battle plan. He decided to put the singers in
the front of the battle singing, **Praise the Lord; for his
mercy endureth for ever** (v. 21).

Now, this is an amazing thing. If you were going to battle
against three nations, it would be common sense to put your
strongest soldiers on the front lines. But they put their singers
up there! They put their musicians up front. They didn't have
any weapons of war, they were believing the word God had
given. They were not expecting to fight — they were believing God for a *supernatural* deliverance.

And when they began to sing and to praise,
the Lord set ambushments against the children
of Ammon, Moab, and mount Seir, which were
come against Judah; and they were smitten.

For the children of Ammon and Moab stood
up against the inhabitants of mount Seir,
utterly to slay and destroy them: and when they

had made an end of the inhabitants of Seir, every one helped to destroy another.

And when Judah came toward the watchtower in the wilderness, they looked unto the multitude, and, behold, they were dead bodies fallen to the earth, and none escaped.

2 Chronicles 20:22-24

Jehoshaphat and his men never had to fight. When the Israelites looked out over the battlefield, it says there was not one man left alive. It took Jehoshaphat's men three days to gather the spoils from the battle. But notice in verse 22 that **when they began to sing and to praise, the Lord set ambushments.** Praise releases God's power and strength to still the enemy. Satan loses his power when God's people begin to praise.

Elisha

Elisha was a man of many miracles. He saw people raised from the dead. (See 2 Kings 4:18-37.) He made the axe head float. (See 2 Kings 6:5,6.) And he multiplied food, just to name a few. (See 2 Kings 4:42-44.)

In 2 Kings 3, we find that Jehoshaphat teamed up with the king of Israel and the king of Edom to fight the Moabites. They traveled for seven days with no food or water for their army or for the animals. The king of Israel was sure that the Lord would deliver them into the hands of the Moabites.

But Jehoshaphat remembered Elisha, went to him, and asked him to pray for their deliverance. Elisha, understanding the power of praise, responded,

As the Lord of hosts liveth, before whom I stand, surely, were it not that I regard the presence of Jehoshaphat the king of Judah, I would not look toward thee, nor see thee.

> But now bring me a minstrel. And it came
> to pass, when the minstrel played, that the
> hand of the Lord came upon him.
>
> 2 Kings 3:14,15

When Elisha surrounded himself with praise, the hand of the Lord came upon him and he gave the three kings the answer they were needing. When Elisha wanted to get a word from God and see the anointing and the power of God manifested, he called for a minstrel, a musician.

This is the background of how a typical church service is conducted. Sometimes we don't think about things — we just do things a certain way because that's the way it has always been done. But somewhere down the line, the Body of Christ understood the power of praise. They understood that praise affects the individual.

Most people enter a church service with their mind on things of this world. They're under pressure and stress from their job or their family. So we begin the service with praise because it changes the individual. It takes their mind off their problems. Praise turns their focus towards God where it belongs.

What Elisha did illustrates the principle behind why our church services are set up the way they are. I quit religion a long time ago. I decided that I'll never do something just because it's traditional. I've analyzed the way we worship God. I went to the Scriptures and said, "God, what's the right way? What should we be doing?" And I came up with the same conclusion: We should begin our services in praise and worship unto God. It prepares people's hearts and it drives the devil off. It releases the anointing of God.

What the Future Holds

Will we ever be problem free? Yes, but not while we're here on this earth. So what do we do in the meantime? We praise God!

> **Rejoice evermore.**
> **Pray without ceasing.**
> **In every thing give thanks: for this is the will of God in Christ Jesus concerning you.**
> **1 Thessalonians 5:16-18**

We must remember the men of the Old Testament, the problems they faced, and how God brought them through. I believe it's safe to assume you don't have three armies planning to attack you, but maybe you are facing trials that seem too great to handle. God's grace is sufficient for you. He is no respecter of persons, and what He did for them, He'll do for you!

Chapter 4

Attitude Is Everything

Proverbs 23:7 says, **As he thinketh in his heart, so is he.** Whatever we're thinking on is the way we're going to be. If we think on discouraging things, we're going to be discouraged. If we think on depressing things, we're going to be depressed. But on the other hand, if we think on God, if we set our mind on the things above, then we are going to be blessed. That's exactly what praise does.

When God created man in His own image (see Genesis 1:27) it meant more than just the physical aspect. It meant more than the fact that we have a spirit, soul, and body. We also have the character of God. I believe that one of the characteristics of God is that He is joyful.

Thou lovest righteousness, and hatest wickedness: therefore God, thy God, hath anointed thee with the oil of gladness above thy fellows.

Psalm 45:7

If we really believe what this scripture says, then Jesus was happier than anyone around Him. God anointed Him with the oil of gladness. Traditionally, that is not the way Jesus is usually presented, but it is exactly what this scripture says. God Himself is a God of praise. God is joyful. God is glad-hearted.

He did not create men to be morbid, sad, or depressed. He did not create us to be gripers and complainers.

Complaining Gets Us Nowhere

When the children of Israel came out of the land of Egypt, it is reported twice that God was so upset with them because of their murmuring and complaining, He was willing to wipe them out and start all over again. From the time the Lord brought them out of Egypt, they griped and complained. God gave them manna from heaven, a supernatural supply of food, yet they griped about it and said, "We hate this light bread! We wish we had something else." (See Numbers 11:6.) Then He gave them meat to eat and they griped about that. (See Numbers 11:32.) They griped about everything the Lord did for them. They did not serve the Lord with joyfulness and gladness of heart for the abundance of all things.

God created man to be thankful. To be depressed, discouraged, unthankful, and unholy is part of the corrupted nature — a result of sin.

This know also, that in the last days perilous times shall come.

For men shall be lovers of their own selves, covetous, boasters, proud, blasphemers, disobedient to parents, unthankful, unholy,

Without natural affection, trucebreakers, false accusers, incontinent, fierce, despisers of those that are good,

Traitors, heady, highminded, lovers of pleasures more than lovers of God;

Having a form of godliness, but denying the power thereof: from such turn away.

2 Timothy 3:1-5

Notice that unthankfulness is put in this list of terrible things that are signs of the end times. Right next to it is unholiness, disobedience to parents, blasphemers, and people who despise everything that is good.

Being thankful is not an option! It's not something that would be nice *if* we felt like doing it. It's the way God made us to be. So, do we *have* to do this? I don't believe we *have* to do anything. God loves us unconditionally. If a person truly puts their faith in the Lord Jesus Christ, they can be born again and will spend eternity with Him. But they are not fulfilling God's will in their life the way they should if they gripe and complain along the way. That is not how God intended us to be. That is not His plan for us.

Do we really want to be all God wants us to be? One of the chief characteristics of a Christian ought to be that of a praiser, someone who gives glory and credit to God, who is thankful and humble and praises God. That ought to be the sign of a Christian. It is not optional. That is the *normal* Christian life.

Abounding in Faith Through Praise

As ye have therefore received Christ Jesus the Lord, so walk ye in him:
Rooted and built up in him, and stablished in the faith, as ye have been taught, abounding therein with thanksgiving.

Colossians 2:6,7

When it says **abounding therein,** the *therein* is referring back to the word *faith*. We abound in faith with thanksgiving. Thanksgiving is a manifestation or a part of praise. We could turn this verse around and say that if we are *not* operating in thanksgiving, we are *not* abounding in faith. That doesn't mean faith isn't there, it means it's not abounding. It is not complete. It's not the highest form of faith.

Anytime we begin to operate in a high form of faith, a Bible-type of faith, praise will be an integral part of that. It's impossible to imagine a person whose faith is complete without thanksgiving. If there is something they are believing for, at the moment it becomes real there is some form of praise.

As an example, say a person was believing and praying for a million dollars for a special need. God supplied their million dollars. Now when that million dollars was placed in their hand, I guarantee you there was some form of praise. Some people may get very emotional, shout, and scream. Others may show their praise in a more subdued fashion. But there would be some reaction of praise. It's impossible to envision our faith being complete without some manifestation of praise when we receive the exact thing we prayed for.

If you're praying for a person to get saved, when you see them accept Jesus, there's going to be some reaction of praise. If you're praying for your children to get right with the Lord, when you see that happen, there's going to be some form of praise.

We can see by observation that when our faith is complete, praise is always there. But instead of waiting for the manifestation to offer praise, we can act on scriptures like Colossians 2:6. By operating in praise, we build up our faith and make our faith complete. We can abound in faith *before* the thing comes. We can increase our faith and operate in a high form of faith by praising God from the moment we see the problem or the need.

Now, I believe it is very important that you understand this, because so much of what people do today in trying to believe God for something is not laced with praise. There is not a lot of praise involved in it. Some people come to me and talk about how they're struggling, they're believing God, they're standing, but they are so depressed and discouraged. If I ask them, "Are you standing in faith? Are you believing God?" they most likely reply, "Man, I'm believing God with everything I've got." But there's no praise. Therefore, they can't be abounding in faith. Praise can be used as an indicator of whether we're really in true Bible faith or whether we're just hoping and trying.

It's very hard to define when a person is just going through the motions and when they're really believing from their heart. We try all kinds of things to describe this. We say that there's a difference between believing in your head and believing in your heart, but it's hard to draw a definitive line between when we're in faith and when we aren't. Sometimes it's even hard for the individual themselves to distinguish this. They can deceive themselves into thinking "I'm standing in faith," but in their heart there's fear that they just aren't willing to acknowledge.

How can we recognize when we're standing in faith? I believe that one of the keys is this area of praise. When we're operating in God's kind of faith, praise will be there. We abound in faith with thanksgiving. If there is no thanksgiving, we are not abounding in faith.

Praise is like a thermometer we can use to take our spiritual temperature and find out where we are in believing God. If there is no praise or if praise is limited, then our faith is limited. When we get to where we're really abounding in praise — praising God as if it was already done — then we know we are beginning to abound in faith and it's just a matter of time until we see the thing that we desire. Praise is a super-important part of faith.

Keeping Our Focus on Jesus

The Scripture says in Hebrews 12:2 that we are supposed to look **unto Jesus the author and finisher of our faith.**

Our faith comes from Jesus. When we are standing on the Word and considering the Word, faith is flowing because faith comes by hearing and hearing by the Word. (See Romans 10:17.) When we are considering Jesus, faith is flowing, because John 1:1 says Jesus is the Word.

When we're looking unto Jesus, which is looking to the Word of God and using it as the basis of our faith, then faith flows. Faith comes from God's Word and beholding what God's Word has to say — considering God's Word and not considering the problem.

On the other hand, unbelief or fear comes from considering things contrary to God's Word. If a doctor tells us we're going to die, and we think on what the doctor says, fear and unbelief are going to come. But if we turn to God's Word and His promises, and think solely on what His Word says, then all we would get would be faith.

Faith has to have Jesus as its object. He is the author and the finisher of our faith, and praise is something that forces us to put our attention on God. When we make a decision to praise God, to discipline ourselves not to gripe, complain, or become negative, we *will* praise God. To follow through with that commitment, we must take our attention off the negative circumstances in our life.

For instance, if the doctor told you you're going to die, and you said, "Well, I'm going to praise God," you wouldn't sit there and say, "Thank-You, Father, that I'm dying. Thank-You that according to this doctor, I'm going to be dead in six months. Thank-You that my wife and kids are going to be destitute." No! There's nothing praiseworthy in that. Those are negative thoughts and are not praiseworthy.

You would follow through with your decision to praise God and say, "I'll praise God in every situation." Psalm 34:1 says, **I will bless the Lord at all times: his praise shall continually be in my mouth.** As you bless the Lord at all times and continuously praise Him, you would take your attention off of the sickness, off of the doctor's report, off of what would happen to your wife and kids, and focus upon God and His promises. You would have to start saying things like, "Father, thank-You that the Word of God says that by the stripes of Jesus I was healed." (See 1 Peter 2:24.) "Father, thank-You that in the Word of God there were people who were in worse shape than I am and You healed them."

You could look at Lazarus. (See John 11:17-44.) You could look at Jairus's daughter and the woman with the issue of blood. (See Luke 8:41-55.) After reading about their situations, you could say, "Praise You, Father, that if You can raise people from the dead, You can surely keep people from dying. Thank-You, Father, that according to the Scripture You heal all of our sicknesses and *all* of our diseases." (See Psalm 103:3.)

In order for you to praise, you've got to get your attention off of the *problem* and onto the *answer.* You've got to get to a place where your faith, your attention, is stayed upon Jesus, the Word of God, and His promises. When you do that, faith works.

Faith really isn't hard, but it is dependent upon your thoughts and your mind-set. If you think on problems, you're going to have unbelief. It doesn't matter what scriptures you've heard, who prays for you, how much you try, or how much you plead with God — if you think on negative circumstances, you're going to be defeated. Doubt and unbelief come through considering things other than the Word of God; faith comes through considering the Word of God.

Prayer or Complaining

If we keep our mind stayed on the Word of God, we will get the results of the Word of God. If we keep our mind stayed on the problem, the problem is going to dominate us.

I have dealt with many women who come to me and complain that their husband is a reprobate. They're trying to pray for him, but they're just beside themselves. They're depressed, they're discouraged, and they say, "What can I do? I've got to have some relief in my home."

Many times I've told these women, "The first thing you need to do is quit praying for your husband."

Most of them react with, "What are you saying? That's terrible! That cannot be from God. I need to pray for my husband." Well, if it was godly prayer, based totally on the Word of God, then I'd say yes to that. But what most people call prayer, is not really prayer — it's complaining.

I heard Charles Capps talk one time about how he was in a real bad situation. He was praying and talking to God about it, and in the middle of his prayer, the Lord said, "What are you doing?"

He said, "Well, I'm praying."

And the Lord told him, "You aren't praying. You're complaining." I really believe that a large portion of what people are calling prayer is not true prayer. It is complaining.

Many of these women praying for their husbands have prayed, "Oh, God, I ask You to save my husband. He beats me. He beats the kids. He beats the dog. He spends our money. He buys booze. He doesn't love me. He...." They'll spend forty-five minutes talking about all the negative things their husband does, and at the end of the prayer, they'll say, "I'm asking You to save him, in Jesus' name. Amen."

They'll spend forty-five minutes talking about the problem and five seconds talking about the answer. Then they wonder why they're depressed, why they're discouraged, and why their prayers haven't been answered. I believe communication is vital to a good marriage and a good prayer life, but we need to learn to communicate good things. We need to repent of those things that don't edify, that will only offend and hurt. Bury them and don't share them with anyone else, even God. Griping is not prayer!

I have seen this so many times when I have preached on forgiveness. One person will go to another person in the service and say, "I want you to know that I forgive you. Right now I am forgiving you for all of the rotten things you've done and said." I've even had people do that to me and I didn't know they were ever upset with me! By doing that, it gave opportunity for another offense to occur.

If you find yourself in a situation like that, desperately needing to forgive another, you should say, "Father, forgive me for taking offense. And forgive Andrew. He didn't mean it. I'm sorry, I ask Your forgiveness. I ask You to take all bitterness away. It's over and I am going to forget it." Then don't speak to anyone about it, because by mentioning it, you put Satan in a position to tempt someone else with an offense.

The same thing is true in a marriage situation. Some things shouldn't even be brought up. Sometimes we need to just repent of our wrong feelings and not go blab about it. Sure, that's communication, but it's not *good* communication. And it's the same thing in prayer. We don't need to pour out our heart, gripe, complain, and tell God how miserable we are. That's not *prayer* — that's *complaining*.

Now there is a place for bearing your heart to the Lord, but it is not the place that most of us have used. It is not forty-five minutes talking about how bad the situation is and five seconds talking about the answer. Maybe we should try spending one minute telling God, "Oh God, this is how I feel," and then start praising Him, expressing our faith, and speaking the answer for forty-five minutes.

That is why I tell a lot of people to quit praying for their mate, because they are focusing on all of those negative things. They would be better off to praise God for what the Word says about their mate. I tell them to start praising God for what they want their mate to be, what they are believing for them to be.

> **For verily I say unto you, That whosoever shall say unto this mountain, Be thou removed, and be thou cast into the sea; and shall not doubt in his heart, but shall believe that those things which he saith shall come to pass; he shall have whatsoever he saith.**
>
> **Therefore I say unto you, What things soever ye desire, when ye pray, believe that ye receive them, and ye shall have them.**
>
> Mark 11:23,24

We can either say what we have or we can have what we say. If we say what we have, looking only at what our mate is constantly doing, then we are just reinforcing those things. We're making the problem grow bigger and bigger in our own mind. It will minister doubt, discouragement, and depression to us. But if we will focus on the answer, then we'll find out that faith will come. We must stay focused on the Word of God and what His Word has to say — then our prayers will be empowered by praise instead of being crushed by continuous negative complaints.

What's the Answer?

How can we keep focused when we're under pressure? When the bills are piling up, it's hard to just close the checkbook and say, "I refuse to think on this." When we have pain in our body, it's hard to ignore that pain. When we see relationships falling apart, how do we keep from dwelling on those things?

I admit that it's not easy to control our minds, but one of the most important things we can do to keep it stayed on the answer instead of the problem is to praise. This is one of the most powerful weapons God has given us. When we are praising God, we have to get into what God is doing. Claiming and praising God for the promises He has given takes our attention off of the negative and immerses us in faith, love, and joy.

You will cease to praise God if you allow your mind to drift back to the negative. But if you make a decision to focus on Him, you can say, "Wait a minute," and go back to praising God. It will take some practice on your part, and it may not happen one time when you decide to do this. It will take some disciplined spiritual exercise.

But strong meat belongeth to them that are of full age, even those who by reason of use have their senses exercised to discern both good and evil.

Hebrews 5:14

Like exercising to build muscles in our body, it takes time and effort to build a consistent attitude of praise. We don't get discouraged if we can't bench press 400 pounds the first day we begin exercising. It takes time to build up to that. But every single time we exert ourselves, we get a little stronger, until one day we reach our goal.

It's the same thing with praise. If you have been very negative, it may take a week. It may take two weeks. It may take longer than that before you begin to see the true benefit of praise. But if you will make this commitment, "God, I'm going to be a person who praises You. I'm going to think on the good things and I refuse to be negative," sooner or later you will exercise yourself unto godliness and reap the benefits.

Rejoice in the Lord alway: and again I say, Rejoice.

Let your moderation be known unto all men. The Lord is at hand.

> **Be careful for nothing; but in every thing**
> **by prayer and supplication with thanksgiving**
> **let your requests be made known unto God.**
> **Philippians 4:4-6**

Paul is talking about praising God and rejoicing in the Lord always. Then he starts talking about prayer. He says, **Be careful for nothing.** In other words, don't be anxious, don't worry about anything, commit **every thing by prayer and supplication with thanksgiving.** Thanksgiving is a part of prayer. We should start our prayer with praise and end our prayer with praise. If we have any problems, we can mention them in between. But even then, we must keep our attention on the answer rather than the problem.

This is exactly the instruction given in Matthew 6, where Jesus talked about what is commonly called the Lord's Prayer. He started it off in verse 9 by saying, **Our Father which art in heaven, Hallowed be thy name.** That's praise! Then He ended it in verse 13 by saying, **For thine is the kingdom, and the power, and the glory, for ever. Amen.** He used what I call a *sandwich technique*. You begin and end with praise. Before you even present your problem, you present the answer. You say, "Praise You, Jesus, that by Your stripes I've been healed." Then you simply mention, "Father, I've got a problem in my body. Thank-You that it's being taken care of." You can mention your problem as long as you are not focused on the problem.

I'm not saying to ignore our problems or not face up to them, but we cannot let the enemy steal our joy. The medical profession has statistics showing that people who are joyful and happy are healthier than people who are morbid, sad, and depressed. Keeping an attitude of praise will keep us filled with His joy.

How We Are to Pray

The effectual fervent prayer of a righteous man availeth much.

James 5:16

I believe that in emphasizing prayer today, we have told people to just *talk* to God. It really doesn't matter what we say; just get there. For an hour or two hours, pray over the situation, and that's all there is to it. We've done our duty. But that's not so. The Scripture calls it an **effectual fervent prayer.** That means that our prayers are effective and fervent. Are we effectively and wholeheartedly communicating with the Lord?

Being effective is praying His Word in faith, and being fervent is our whole heart filled with praise and thanksgiving unto Him. We will see results when we pray this type of prayer. Complaining will get us nowhere, but praise will open heaven's gates!

Chapter 5

Wake Up!

I beseech you therefore, brethren, by the mercies of God, that ye present your bodies a living sacrifice, holy, acceptable unto God, which is your reasonable service.

And be not conformed to this world: but be ye transformed by the renewing of your mind, that ye may prove what is that good, and acceptable, and perfect, will of God.

Romans 12:1,2

There are two types of problems — problems we have personally and problems in the world that directly or indirectly affect us. As I have said throughout this book, finding the answer to any problem begins with praise. When you praise God you step into His presence and find the answer. But when you do not praise Him, you step away from Him and all you see is the problem.

Stepping Away From God

For the wrath of God is revealed from heaven against all ungodliness and unrighteousness of men, who hold the truth in unrighteousness;

Because that which may be known of God is manifest in them; for God hath shown it unto them.

> For the invisible things of him from the creation of the world are clearly seen, being understood by the things that are made, even his eternal power and Godhead; so that they are without excuse:
>
> Because that, when they knew God, they glorified him not as God, neither were thankful; but became vain in their imaginations and their foolish heart was darkened.
>
> Professing themselves to be wise, they became fools,
>
> And changed the glory of the uncorruptible God into an image made like to corruptible man, and to birds, and fourfooted beasts, and creeping things.
>
> Wherefore God also gave them up to uncleanness through the lusts of their own hearts, to dishonour their own bodies between themselves.
>
> **Romans 1:18-24**

Paul is saying that every person who's ever been created has an intuitive knowledge of God. But because they do not worship Him, because they do not glorify Him as God, and because they are not thankful, they become fools. They enter into idolatry and from there progress into all types of perversion.

I want you to notice the progression. First of all, every person in verses 18 through 20 has an intuitive knowledge of God so that **they are without excuse,** in verse 20. Then he shows you how this stepping away from God starts — they don't glorify Him as God. That's talking about praise. They don't give the praise and recognition to God that is due unto Him, neither are they thankful.

Then it says they **became vain in their imaginations.** The next step is that their foolish heart is darkened. Once a person's heart begins to harden towards God, according to Mark, chapter 8, they become spiritually retarded. That's my own terminology, but that's what the results of a hardened heart are. It takes away our ability to think rationally. So one of the things that will keep us from stepping away from God is giving praise and glory unto God, and being thankful.

Ruling Over Our Feelings

Some people say, "But I just don't feel like praising God." Who cares how we feel? We need to do it because God's Word says to do it.

Others may say, "But wait, I didn't choose to be discouraged, it just happened. It's just the way I feel. I can't help it."

To let our emotions and feelings rule us is very, very immature. I say this in love — it cuts me the same as it cuts anyone else. We were raised that our feelings should dominate us, but that's not right. Just because we *feel* depressed doesn't mean we have to *be* depressed. I have thoughts of depression come at me, but I choose to reject them. I choose to build myself up and encourage myself in the Lord. Feelings are to be enjoyed when they are good, and they are to be rejected when they are bad. Emotions are never to dictate to us; we are to control them.

Psychology has told us, "Don't suppress your feelings. Let them all out." Now I agree that it isn't healthy to store things up on the inside and simmer and brood over them. But when we have negative emotions, instead of letting them out, we should reject them and choose instead the positive emotions of praising and glorifying God. If we would choose to do that, we would experience a new power in our lives. Our minds would be stayed on God, and our faith would abound on the inside of us.

Faith Isn't Magic

Many people try to use their faith to get rid of all their problems. To a degree, we can do that — we can avoid a lot of problems by just walking in the Word of God. Some of our problems are direct demonic attacks, and we can overcome those things through the Word. But we're never going to avoid every problem.

If we walk in health 100 percent of the time and never have any physical problems, and if we walk in prosperity and never have any financial problems, I can promise this: Satan will have someone come along who rubs us the wrong way. And even if no one rubs us the wrong way and we get along great with everyone we meet, *some* problem will rise up against us because we don't live in a perfect world.

If your idea of walking in peace and victory is having all of your problems removed, you'll never obtain that. You've got to realize that it doesn't matter what the devil throws against you, God says you can prosper in the midst of it. You can praise God and keep your mind stayed on Him. That's the way to handle the pressures of life and maintain our Christian walk.

Guided by Circumstances

The reason so many people are fighting depression today is because everything in the natural world is geared towards being negative and depressed. The news media reports all of the negative news. They don't tell you the good things, only the bad. If we listen to the world, it would appear that we are *surrounded* by horrible situations. And if we allow ourselves to be dominated by the thinking of this world, we are going to have depression among us.

But our circumstances don't make us the way we are — that's *our* choice. We can choose to react to our circumstances and be depressed or discouraged, or we can choose to look beyond our circumstances to God's faithfulness towards us and be blessed.

I remember when the United States entered the Gulf War. Some members of Congress and many people in this country were saying it was going to be a bloodbath for the United States. Some predicted an excess of 20,000 to 30,000 U.S. lives would be lost. Others predicted that we were going to be wiped out by all of the Russian tanks in the Persian Gulf. Very few people boldly disagreed with those negative comments.

It caused fear and concern in America's people. We entered the war very apprehensively. But in retrospect, it was the most minimal loss of life in the history of the United States. Our equipment proved superior over anything that the Iraqis had. So where were all these people that a year earlier had made those terrible predictions? They should have been voted out of office. They were totally out of touch and missed it big time. But sad to say, many of them are still in office, still making their negative predictions, and people are still listening to them.

The Slant of the Media

The news media is slanted against reporting things from a Christian perspective. The truth is, I believe we are experiencing the greatest revival that has ever hit the United States. Many people would disagree with me, but I'm basing this on what the Word of God says and what I'm seeing in the Body of Christ today. I'll admit there are plenty of problems out there. Satan's crowd has gotten more vocal and more visible than they've ever been. If you focus on those things, you could make a real case for America being in total moral decay. But when you really look at it from God's perspective, I believe you'll find out that it's different than the way the news media has presented it.

Take the gay rights movement for example. The homosexuals have gained tremendous attention just from television. People are hearing so much about AIDS, equal rights for gay couples, and so on, that it has developed a mentality in people that the homosexuals really have become an accepted part of the community — or at least they are headed that way. Yet I heard a survey in 1992 on radio station KPBC in Dallas that gave the following statistics: in 1960, 68 percent of the American population thought homosexuality was wrong. They didn't just express that it wasn't their preference, they thought it was wrong for anyone. They believed that it was a perversion — it wasn't normal. In 1992, guess what the percentage was. Most people would say, "Well, it was probably less than 50 percent." That's certainly the reaction I had. But the statistics in the survey showed that in 1992, 75 percent of the American public thought homosexuality was wrong — that it was a perversion. That was a 7 percent increase from 1960. We are more moral in that area today than we were in the sixties. Yet, that's not the perception most people have, because the news media is not being fair and honest. They are painting a deceptive picture.

As another example, the National Organization for Women (NOW) gets quoted constantly. Every time there is an abortion right's issue or a pro-choice issue, newspeople go to that group of women to get their views because they are supposed to be spokespersons for women. There's somewhere around 200,000 women involved in NOW — less than most organizations that have any type of political clout.

But Concerned Women for America, a Christian group organized by Beverly LaHaye, has over 600,000 women in its organization. They have three times more representation than NOW, yet you never hear them quoted on political issues.

Recently, there was a rally at the Capitol that drew literally hundreds of thousands of people protesting abortion. The newspaper covering the story had a picture of about a dozen people standing with pro-abortion placards on the front page! By listening to the media, it would be easy to think, *Man, things are falling apart. It's really a terrible world we live in!* What a depressing thought. But the truth is, God is doing great things today. There are more born-again, Spirit-filled people per capita in the United States today than there has ever been in the history of this country. There are more people praying and seeking God than ever before.

There Is Hope

In my own personal life, I know at least thirty-eight people who have either been raised from the dead or who have raised someone from the dead. I have a friend in Salt Lake City who has raised eight people from the dead personally. One of my staff members, Don Krow, saw his daughter raised from the dead after he prayed for her.

I conducted a meeting in Kansas City and two people who had been raised from the dead stood up. I had been there when it happened to one of them eleven years before this. At that time during my message, the pastor and some of the people in the church went out and prayed for him. He was gone for forty-five minutes, but then he was raised from the dead and brought back in! The reason I say this is to bring up the point that only eight people in the Bible were raised from the dead.

It's awesome to think that one person knows at least thirty-eight people — nearly five times the number as recorded in the Bible — that were raised from the dead. That's a reason to be excited! Something is happening in our day. I believe God is on the move. There are great things happening in America!

Satan Is Losing

In traveling to different churches around the nation, I've been to at least a dozen places that say, "Man, this is the occult capital of the United States." Now, they can't all be the occult *capital!* They can't *all* have all the satanic power. But if they see any satanic ability whatsoever, they want to say it's the occult. Somehow or another, it's exciting to say, "We're in this battle! We need to stand strong against this." The truth is, Satan is losing big time. I'm not saying Satan hasn't made some great inroads and won some battles, but God's winning the war.

There are two sides to this coin. God's kingdom is getting stronger and Satan's kingdom is getting stronger. How can this be? Because all of the middle ground is leaving. People who were just kind of moral but weren't really seeking God are becoming either hot or cold. We can focus on the cold. We can look only at the negative and paint a very bleak picture, or we can focus on the positive. There is a lot of positive out there. And there's a lot of positive in your own situation if you would just wake up and see it!

Choosing Freedom

We need to wake up! We need to jar ourselves and recognize that we have become negative. We have become murmurers and complainers. It's not our hormones that make us depressed, it's what we set our mind on. It's our stinking thinking. If we would change our attitude and begin to praise God in every situation like Habakkuk and like Paul and Silas did in the dungeon, we would experience the life of God. We can choose to be blessed. We have a choice in the matter.

I was in England in 1990 conducting some meetings and a woman who had just gotten out of a mental hospital was brought there by a family member. She was suicidal and had tried to kill herself a number of times. Now I didn't know any of these things about her, but I knew God was ministering to her. I called her out and began to pray for her. As I did, the Lord showed me that she had been mentally unstable and I told her that if she wanted to be free, she could. It was her choice. She could be depressed and guilt-ridden, or she could choose to believe that she was forgiven. This woman was already born again and was still experiencing these problems.

The next day, she called the pastor and told him she woke up and felt depressed again, but she chose to start praising God, and said she had been doing great. She called back two more times the week I was there and said she had done the same thing with great results. It's been years since then, and that woman is so set free, she's been on television and radio, holding seminars and talking to people about how to be delivered. This woman was incapable of even functioning and now she's helping other people because she realized her emotional state was a choice — it was her decision. She's a tremendous testimony.

If you're depressed today, you chose to be depressed. You may not have sat down and said, "I want to be depressed," but you chose to think on things that made you depressed.

> **Finally, brethren, whatsoever things are true, whatsoever things are honest, whatsoever things are just, whatsoever things are pure, whatsoever things are lovely, whatsoever things are of good report; if there be any virtue, and if there be any praise, think on these things.**
>
> **Philippians 4:8**

If we would choose to think on things that are honest, pure, and lovely, we would experience freedom from depression. If we would stay spiritually-minded, we would have life and peace. But if we are carnally-minded, that is death.

For to be carnally minded is death; but to be spiritually minded is life and peace.

Romans 8:6

Being spiritually-minded is being Word-minded. John 6:63 says, **The words that I speak unto you, they are spirit, and they are life.** If you're having anything other than life and peace, you haven't kept your mind stayed on the Word of God.

How do you have life and peace? Praise puts your attention on God. Praise makes you aware of what God is doing. As you stay your mind on God, you're going to have life and peace. The peace of God will keep your heart and mind through Christ Jesus. God will keep you in perfect peace when your mind is fixed upon Him.

Set your affection on things above, not on things on the earth.

Colossians 3:2

We don't have to think on the things of this world. We can set our affection on things above. And when we set our affection — our full attention — on God and what He's doing, our problems are supernaturally swallowed up by our Answer!

Chapter 6

Living Free

We praise God because He is worthy of our praise, but the results of our praise affect us tremendously! Now, we've got to make sure that our motives are pure in this. We shouldn't worship God only because it's going to benefit us. If it never benefited us, we still should worship God because He is worthy to be praised. But I promise you, you cannot outgive God. When you begin to give glory and praise unto Him, He is going to multiply it back unto you.

Give, and it shall be given unto you; good measure, pressed down, and shaken together, and running over, shall men give into your bosom.

Luke 6:38

We most often use this scripture and relate it to financial giving. But if you will start blessing Him, He's going to bless you more than you've ever blessed Him. His love will be so manifest in your life, that you will be filled with all the fullness of God.

We Are His Temple

David wanted to build a temple for the Lord, but the Lord told him not to do it himself. He said that He would let his son, Solomon, build Him a temple, which he did. (See 1 Chronicles 22:6-12.) Even though David was forbidden to build the temple, he did establish a tabernacle. He brought the ark of the covenant into Jerusalem and ordered that worship was to continually take place in the tabernacle.

> **Moreover four thousand were porters; and four thousand praised the Lord with the instruments which I made, said David, to praise therewith.**
>
> **And David divided them into courses among the sons of Levi, namely, Gershon, Kohath, and Merari.**
>
> **1 Chronicles 23:5,6**

David put them into different work shifts so that twenty-four hours a day there was praise going up to God. The only job for four thousand people was to praise God. What would happen if churches today were to designate four hundred people that were paid just to worship and praise the Lord? I am sure many would criticize that because we just don't put that kind of priority on praise. Yet this is what the whole tabernacle was all about. David designated these singers to offer worship unto God, twenty-four hours a day, through musical instruments, singing, and praising.

> **By him therefore let us offer the sacrifice of praise to God continually, that is, the fruit of our lips giving thanks to his name.**
>
> **Hebrews 13:15**

As New Testament believers, *we* are the temple of the Lord. We have churches that we go to, but they are just places to meet. The temple of the Lord is us, and our temple should be worshipping and praising God twenty-four hours a day. A continual sacrifice means we praise Him not only when we feel like it, but just because God is good. David was constantly praising God. That's one of the things that made him a man after God's own heart.

He Inhabits Our Praises

Let them praise his name in the dance: let them sing praises unto him with the timbrel and harp.

For the Lord taketh pleasure in his people: he will beautify the meek with salvation.

Psalm 149:3,4

But thou art holy, O thou that inhabitest the praises of Israel.

Psalm 22:3

The Lord thy God in the midst of thee is mighty; he will save, he will rejoice over thee with joy; he will rest in his love, he will joy over thee with singing.

Zephaniah 3:17

God gets pleasure out of us. He inhabits our praises. Those scriptures show a God who loves us — not a God who pities us or has a sense of obligation towards us. He joys over us with singing!

Many years ago, the Lord allowed Jamie to see into the spiritual realm and she saw angels in the building dancing over us as we praised the Lord. At first I thought, *How could this be? Who are we to think the angels of God could be dancing and rejoicing with us?* Then the Lord reminded me of Zephaniah 3:17. When we begin to worship Him, it touches the heart of God and all of heaven goes to dancing and praising God. There is rejoicing in heaven when we praise God.

Praise Takes Us Into His Presence

It came even to pass, as the trumpeters and singers were as one, to make one sound to be heard in praising and thanking the Lord; and

> when they lifted up their voice with the trumpets and cymbals and instruments of music, and praised the Lord, saying, For he is good; for his mercy endureth for ever: that then the house was filled with a cloud, even the house of the Lord;
>
> So that the priests could not stand to minister by reason of the cloud: for the glory of the Lord had filled the house of God.

> 2 Chronicles 5:13,14

David had designated four thousand people to praise God constantly and Solomon followed that same example when he dedicated the temple. As they began to praise God, the glory of the Lord filled the house so that it literally knocked them to their faces. The power and the glory of God filled the house as they praised and worshipped Him.

God inhabits the praises of His people. A person who is not praising God is a person who is not really entering into the gates and the courts of the Lord. Now I'm not saying that if we aren't praising God, we aren't born again and the power of God isn't resident on the inside of us, but it's never going to be manifested until we begin to glorify and praise Him. That is one of the most important things we can do.

> Whoso offereth praise glorifeth me: and to him that ordereth his conversation aright will I shew the salvation of God.

> Psalm 50:23

Ordering our conversation aright means we are praising God and giving the glory due unto Him.

Praise Keeps Us Humble

> For God resisteth the proud, and giveth grace to the humble. Humble yourselves

therefore under the mighty hand of God, that he may exalt you in due time.

1 Peter 5:5,6

Praising God and giving thanks unto Him makes us humble. A person who is full of praise and thankfulness is a person who is constantly acknowledging that it is not their own effort that is producing blessings and prosperity in their life.

Praise reminds us Who our source is. A person who is not praising God is a proud person — a person caught up in their own things.

First Timothy 3:6 says that if we get lifted up with pride, we will fall into the condemnation of the devil. That's the inroad Satan has into our life.

Pride can be defined many different ways. It is not only thinking we're better than someone else, but in its simplest terms, it is self-centeredness. One can have a very low self-esteem, but if they are self-centered, they are in pride. They are not relying on God as their source. They are self-consumed. Praise keeps us in humility towards God. A person who is thankful is a humble person — one who acknowledges that it is not their own power that has produced blessings in their life, but rather it's God who has blessed them. A person who will give praise and thanks unto God is constantly remembering that God is their source.

When Moses began to bring the children of Israel into the promised land, he gave them these instructions right before his death.

And it shall be, when the Lord thy God shall have brought thee into the land which he sware unto thy fathers, to Abraham, to Isaac, and to Jacob, to give thee great and goodly cities, which thou buildest not,

And houses full of all good things, which thou filledst not, and wells digged, which thou

diggedst not, vineyards and olive trees, which thou plantedst not; when thou shalt have eaten and be full;

Then beware lest thou forget the Lord, which brought thee forth out of the land of Egypt, from the house of bondage.

Deuteronomy 6:10-12

He warned the people not to forget the Lord and to praise Him for all the good things they had. He gave explicit directions that praise was to be an integral part of them remembering their roots — remembering where they had come from.

Praise Reveals His Love

That Christ may dwell in your hearts by faith; that ye, being rooted and grounded in love,

May be able to comprehend with all saints what is the breadth, and length, and depth, and height;

And to know the love of Christ, which passeth knowledge, that ye might be filled with all the fulness of God.

Ephesians 3:17-19

He desires to have an *intimate* relationship with us. As we begin to love Him with all of our heart, mind, soul, and strength, we'll see that intimate, personal relationship develop. We'll have a revelation of just how much God loves us. The love of God will be shed abroad in our heart. It will be poured out on us.

But many times we're not clear on how to have that intimate relationship. We think we have to earn it or work for it. *If I do this for God or if I do that, then all of these things will happen.* No, the truth is that God already loves you without you doing anything. Thank Him for that love, remembering the great things He has done for you.

When we experience the love of God, we'll start praising Him more; and as we praise Him more, we'll experience more of the love of God. It's a never ending cycle.

Everything comes from love. Do you need more faith? Galatians 5:6 tells us that faith works by love. If you need more faith then you need more love manifested — a revelation of His love. How do you get it? By praising God. As you begin to love Him, release your love towards God, and enter into this personal relationship, the love of God will abound in your life.

Praise Will Exchange Negative for Positive

I've seen people dying in the hospital that physically should have recovered, but their negative emotions affected their physical body. We can see how our emotional and spiritual well-being can affect us in a lot of ways. We can usually identify a person who is stressed by looking at their face. It can affect their hair, their skin, and their eyes. I believe it was Mary, Queen of Scots, who had a full head of red hair, and the night before she was executed it is said that her hair turned snow white overnight because of the worry and fear of being beheaded the next day. Our emotions can directly affect our physical body, and one of the ways Satan tries to devour us is with bad health.

An attitude of praise and thanksgiving will stop many of Satan's attacks against us. Proverbs 17:22 says, **A merry heart doeth good like a medicine.** It is a front line of defense against physical problems, and I believe the same thing is true in the area of finances. A person who has a positive attitude and is praising God will have creative ideas, whereas a negative person will not have creative ideas.

I have prayed for people and God has given me a special word, a creative word, for their situation. I'll tell them, "Here's what you can do." But as I share it with them, they are so discouraged that they just don't have any vision. They're in a survival mode. They can't think about growth or about getting out and doing something — they're just trying to survive.

Once a person gets that kind of attitude, it's very critical because they wouldn't receive the answer if God gave it to them. They just aren't receptive to it. They see themselves as a certain way or in what they feel is a hopeless situation and because of their attitude, they aren't ever going to come out of it.

For as he thinketh in his heart, so is he.

Proverbs 23:7

If you see yourself poor, if you see yourself a failure, then that's the way you're going to be. But praise will make you see yourself differently. Praise will stop the negative attitudes that Satan loves and feeds on. It will drive Satan away and in the absence of Satan's depression and discouragement, creative ideas will come to you.

A lady in one of my Bible studies was praying about her financial situation, and God showed her that she already had the answer in her hand. She had been making a special kind of clay for her children to play with that was nontoxic, colorfast, pleasant smelling, and couldn't get in the carpet and cause problems. The Lord told her to market it. In just a couple of years, her creative idea became a two million dollar business.

Those kind of things are just a thought away from anyone. But it's the negativism we harbor that keeps us from receiving these words from God. Satan has blinded people from God's answer. How do we overcome that? Praise will change it. Praise will not only change our attitude, but it will literally drive Satan and his deception away. Praise will bring the anointing of God on our lives, and 2 Corinthians 3:17 says,

Where the Spirit of the Lord is, there is liberty — freedom. This is a freedom only God can give. But He can give it only if we enter His gates with thanksgiving and come into His courts with praise.

Living free is available to us at all times and in all situations if we continually praise God. It's just that simple! Because when we praise Him, the Holy Spirit fills our whole being, surrounds us with God's love and grace, and whatever troubles we have fade into the background in light of His glory. Now that's the way I want to live!

Chapter 7

Experiencing Eternal Life

The secular world has reduced everyone to a few numbers — a computer number, a social security number, or maybe a credit card number. We're finding impersonalization on nearly every level of society. If I call my credit card company, I get a computer that tells me, "If you want this option, push this button. For another option, push another button," and I can do my entire transaction without ever talking to a live person. In the name of efficiency, I've become just another number. As a result, there's no need for relationship. Why should I speak to a live person when a computer can do the task more efficiently? But we need relationship — that's what people are hungry for.

The True Purpose of Salvation

For God so loved the world, that he gave his only begotten Son, that whosoever believeth in him should not perish, but have everlasting life.
John 3:16

Most people are so familiar with this verse that they honestly don't know what it says. We take this verse and teach that Jesus came and died for our sins so we wouldn't perish.

Basically, that has been the message of the Church. We have preached that if you don't want to go to hell, you need to accept Jesus as your Savior. And even though those are true statements, that's not the message the New Testament church preached.

The Gospel means good news, or literally, glad tidings. Now it's true that if a person doesn't accept Jesus as the payment for their sins they will go to hell, but that's not good news. It's true, but it's not good news. The good news is that even though you deserve to go to hell, Jesus paid for your sins. Why? So you would not perish *but* have everlasting life. The real emphasis of John 3:16 should be that Jesus came to bring us *everlasting life*.

Sin was not the real purpose of Jesus coming to this earth. He did not come primarily to forgive mankind of their sins. Jesus came to bring man into eternal life. He came to bring us into relationship with God. It just so happened that sin was the obstacle, the barrier, that stood between us and God, and it had to be dealt with. Man couldn't overcome his own sinfulness, so Jesus died for our sins. Sin was moved out of the way so we could have an intimate relationship with God.

Eternal Life Is Now

If a person only gets their sins forgiven and knows Jesus is their Savior, but they don't enter into an intimate relationship with God, they are missing out on what eternal life is all about. Most people think eternal life is living forever — never dying. But the Bible says that everyone is going to live forever in the sense that no one ceases to exist. (See Matthew 25:46.) We will either live forever with God or forever with Satan in the lake of fire, which is what's called the *second death*. (See Revelation 20:14 and 21:8.)

> These things have I written unto you that believe on the name of the Son of God; that ye may know that ye have eternal life, and that ye may believe on the name of the Son of God.
>
> **1 John 5:13**
>
> And this is life eternal, that they might know thee the only true God, and Jesus Christ, whom thou hast sent.
>
> **John 17:3**

Eternal life is not something that is going to happen when we go to heaven. Eternal life is something that is a present-tense reality. Eternal life is *knowing* God. The word *know* is the same word that was used in Genesis 4:1 when it said that **Adam *knew* Eve his wife; and she conceived, and bare Cain.** It was a term used many times in the Old Testament describing an intimate sexual relationship. So when it says, **this is life eternal, that they might know thee the only true God, and Jesus Christ, whom thou hast sent** — it's saying that eternal life is an intimate, personal relationship with God. That is what Jesus came to purchase. That is the whole purpose of salvation.

As I said earlier, God didn't just pity us and make a way so we wouldn't die and go to hell, but He loved us enough to take away the sin so we could enter into personal relationship with Him. Christianity is based on relationship, not rules and regulations. It is not just a doctrine. Other religions of the world have a doctrine. Many of them have moral codes of conduct that are actually equal to or stricter than Christianity. But the thing they're missing is a personal relationship with God. No other religion on the face of the earth can offer that. Jesus defined eternal life as intimate relationship with God.

I got a letter several years ago from a woman in the Huntsville, Texas, prison who was in solitary confinement for a severe crime and not eligible for parole for twenty years.

After she entered prison, she had a real genuine experience with the Lord and was born again. She said she knew for sure that she was born again, and that if she was to die she would go to heaven. That was not her problem.

However she felt like her whole life had been wasted. The family that she grew up in had been totally disgraced by her conduct. She had ruined her own personal family life. She was married and had kids and now her husband had divorced her. Her kids were without a mother because she was in the state penitentiary, and she had also interfered in another family — her victim's family. Many people had been affected by her crime and many lives ruined. So this woman felt like all she had ever been was a problem to people. She didn't have cell mates because she was in solitary confinement, so she didn't get to meet other people and felt she couldn't redeem her life by sharing the Gospel with others. Now she was born again, but being in prison, she felt she was a leech on society.

This woman was so totally depressed and discouraged that she was saying, "God, take me home. I want to die. I want to go home. There's no purpose in me living here. All I'm doing is occupying space, breathing air someone else could be using."

She felt totally useless because of the mentality that says our net worth to God is related to exactly what we can do for Him — how we can produce. But she heard me on the radio and wrote to me. She explained the past situation, and then she said, "But now I understand that God loves me not just for what I can do for Him, but God loves me and I can bless Him. I can minister back unto Him. I can make my life count. I can love God. Now I have a purpose for living. The twenty years until my parole will seem like no time now because I can minister unto God. God is blessed by my praise."

That's what eternal life is all about. Our relationship with God has to be our foundation — the priority above anything and everything else. That woman was experiencing more salvation, more freedom, and more liberty than most Christians who have never been in jail. She was forced to put her attention on the Lord and recognize that this was all she could offer Him.

The Effectiveness of the Early Church

That which we have seen and heard declare we unto you, that ye also may have fellowship with us: and truly our fellowship is with the Father, and with his Son Jesus Christ.

And these things write we unto you, that your joy may be full.

1 John 1:3,4

The early New Testament church had a personal relationship with God, which is why their message was so effective. It is a historical fact that in the thirty years after the resurrection of Jesus, the New Testament church evangelized their known world. Now that is an awesome statement! These people didn't have the advantages of radio and television, cassette tapes, or the modern means of transportation that we have. They were handicapped in nearly every physical area compared to where we are today, yet they made a greater impact on their world than we're making on ours.

We're dumping billions and billions of dollars into preaching the Gospel — a great effort — yet a group of unlearned, uneducated people without our technological advances and without the ability to travel like we can made a greater impact. I believe you can boil the difference down to the fact that people were drawn to their message because of their personal relationship with the Father.

Look at what their message was — God loves you and created you for fellowship. They weren't preaching hell, damnation, and repentance, which is the modern-day message. They were preaching that God created mankind to have relationship with Him.

The people would ask, "How can I have it?"

And the apostles would reply, "Repent of your sins, receive Jesus and the forgiveness that's already offered. It's there for you."

Satisfying Our Spiritual Hunger

The apostles brought people to relationship with God, and that's what people are hungry for today. There's a desire, a drive, on the inside of every person for deep, intimate, personal relationship, but it's been so perverted today. Many don't recognize this drive, and they try to fulfill it in sexual relationships or drug abuse or other things. When they find out that's not where it's at, then they go into some other kind of perversion, thinking that the little zing they get out of it will satisfy that hunger, but it doesn't.

The only thing that is going to satisfy a person's hunger in their heart is a personal relationship with the Lord. Many Christians may not get into immorality, adultery, homosexuality, or other perversions, but they try to fill that longing on the inside with *service*. They become so busy and so preoccupied with *doing* the Lord's work, that they numb themselves to their own hunger. That's not what it's all about.

What if you were stranded on a desert island, and could no longer *do* anything for the Lord? What if all you had was just you and God — there was no one else to minister to and nothing to do? How would your relationship be?

How Do We Measure Up?

I believe that the vast majority of Christians are consumed with *asking* God for things — not *ministering unto* God. If we

FELLOWSHIP OF BELIEVERS

New Location
20401 S. Western Avenue
Olympia Fields, IL 60461

A TIME OF BREAKTHROUGH

EVERY:

SUNDAY AT 2:00 PM

THURSDAY AT 7:00 PM

For More Information Please Contact
Bishop Grey Jacobs   Pastor Tina Jacobs
Phone: 708 · 481 · 3766

Email: fob_jacobs@comcast.net

Service being held at Assumption Greek Orthodox Church

JEAN M™

myjeanm.com

Wedding Accessories and Invitations
To receive your free catalog, mail this card
or call toll free: 1.800.677.8595

Requestor's Information

Name

Address

City, State, Zip

Phone   Event Date

E-mail Address

Send to a Friend

Name

Address

City, State, Zip

Phone

E-mail Address

Catalog requested by:

☐ Bride   ☐ Groom

☐ Other _____

JEAN M™

PO Box 330
Sugar City, ID 83448-0330

Visit our website at
www.elegantbride.com

BUSINESS REPLY MAIL

FIRST-CLASS MAIL   PERMIT NO. 108   BOONE IA

POSTAGE WILL BE PAID BY ADDRESSEE

ELEGANT

bride

PO BOX 37752
BOONE IA 50037-2752

The American Wedding

Album

The American Stationery Co., Inc.

300 N. Park Avenue

Peru, Indiana 46970-1701

The American Wedding

Album®

Mail this card today, or CALL TOLL FREE 1-800-428-0379
for a **FREE** Color Catalog and FREE Invitation Samples.

OR, REACH US ON-LINE AT:
www.theamericanwedding.com

Name _____

Address _____ Apt. #

City _____ State _____ Zip

Wedding Date: _____ E-Mail _____

Phone _____
        Day   Evening   E052B

were to break Christians into two groups, carnal and spiritual, carnal Christians spend the majority of their prayer time asking God specifically for *things*. It may be for physical needs, financial needs, or emotional needs, but it's *things*. Spiritual Christians who spend most of their prayer time interceding for others to have things, emotional, physical, or financial, are still asking God for *things*.

But if we were stranded on a desert island and all of our asking for things for ourselves or for others was taken away, what would our personal relationship with the Lord be like? What if we didn't have to practice spiritual warfare and the only ones present were us and God? Would we *know* God? What if it were us in the Garden of Eden communing with God all day? How would we measure up?

If we took away all the time we spend asking for things or interceding for others and boiled it down to how much time we spend ministering unto God and loving Him, many Christians would come up short. However, that should be the bulk of our prayer.

But seek ye first the kingdom of God, and his righteousness; and all these things shall be added unto you.

Matthew 6:33

If we would put the Lord first, love Him, and minister unto Him, we wouldn't have to spend so much time asking for things — they would be added unto us.

Eternal life is relationship — a close, intimate, personal relationship with God. We need to make that the focal point of our lives. I can say from my own personal life that it's something I constantly have to deal with. I don't ever just make a decision in this area and never again have trouble with it. Constantly, I have to war against the things of this world that come in, want to occupy my time, and keep me from a personal relationship with God.

It may be even more difficult for ministers, because it's so easy to justify not spending much personal time with the Lord because what we're *doing* is so important. But when we recognize that our ministry unto the Lord has such great eternal value, it elevates our relationship with the Father to such a high priority that we can nearly justify letting everything else go.

Our personal relationship with the Lord keeps everything in its proper order — spiritually and naturally. One pastor was telling me that it had been four or five years since he and his family had taken any time off. They needed to get away from the ministry and spend time with the Lord and with each other. So they planned their vacation, and on the day they were supposed to leave, someone in their church died. Because he was the pastor, they felt they had an obligation to stay and minister to the family. So they did. They canceled their vacation. It's easy to get busy and that involved in the ministry, but we have to realize we have a priority to our family — and even beyond that, we have a priority to God.

The Lord spoke to me that if I ever get to where I am more concerned about ministering to people than I am about ministering to Him, I'm going to actually decrease the length of my ministry. I'll become ineffective. The very thing that has caused God to anoint me and use me to be a blessing to other people is dependent upon my personal relationship with Him. If I get so busy ministering to other people that I have no time for God, I'll shorten this ministry and actually reach fewer people. Even the Lord Himself would separate with His disciples and run away from the multitude because they needed to rest.

To keep things in perspective, sometimes we've got to turn down opportunities to minister to people. We can't put off our personal time with the Lord. That develops and strengthens our relationship with Him — that is where we experience *eternal life*.

Chapter 8

Armed and Dangerous

We established in chapter one that praise is strength. Jesus quoted Psalm 8:2 to the Pharisees as He entered Jerusalem and called *perfected praise* the same thing as *ordained strength*. This strength stops the enemy. It stills the avenger. And one of the greatest benefits of praise is that it is such a powerful weapon against the devil.

There is a tremendous amount of teaching on spiritual warfare, and I believe that there's a lot of truth out there, but in my estimation, there has been a lot of abuse too. I have seen many people get into what they are calling spiritual warfare, when actually it's rather depressing. They are fighting with the devil and are spending more time with the devil than they are with God. That's not right.

Please don't misunderstand what I am saying. There is a place for fighting against the devil and resisting him, but I am saying that praise is one of the most powerful weapons we have. It literally makes Satan flee in terror when we begin to praise God.

Walking in Knowledge

To deliver such an one unto Satan for the destruction of the flesh, that the spirit may be saved in the day of the Lord Jesus.

1 Corinthians 5:5

To whom ye forgive any thing, I forgive also: for if I forgave any thing, to whom I forgave it, for your sakes forgave I it in the person of Christ;

Lest Satan should get an advantage of us: for we are not ignorant of his devices.

2 Corinthians 2:10,11

In 1 Corinthians, Paul instructed the Corinthian church how to discipline a man who had been with his father's wife. He told them that they were to turn him over to Satan. In 2 Corinthians, he told the people that the man's punishment was enough — he had repented and they should receive him back.

Unforgiveness is one inroad that Satan has into our life. Paul is saying that if we are ignorant of Satan's devices, he has an opportunity to come against us. Even though these scriptures are talking about unforgiveness, the principle is that if we're ignorant of how Satan operates, then it can give the enemy an opportunity against us.

In order to recognize Satan and his devices, we need to understand that he is totally dominated by self-centeredness. He wants everything for himself. Anything that draws people's attention away from God is a device of the devil. It doesn't always have to be something we call outright sin. He's not always going to get people to worship him directly, but he can get them *not* to worship God if they don't know his schemes.

The best offense against the ways of the enemy is to give people *knowledge*. Knowledge is power. When we begin to understand how Satan attacks us and how he operates, then we can deal with those areas.

The Devices of the Enemy

I could write a very lengthy list of all the devices of the enemy. But suffice it to say that every single trick Satan has for believers is designed to keep us from praising and worshipping God. He sees the power that it releases in our life. He certainly doesn't want us to prosper and be in good health. Most importantly, he doesn't want the Lord to be worshipped. If he can get us to stop praising God, we have taken a step towards the devil. When we are praising God, we are defeating the plans of the devil and fulfilling the purpose of our creation.

> **Be sober, be vigilant; because your adversary the devil, as a roaring lion, walketh about, seeking whom he may devour:**
>
> **Whom resist stedfast in the faith, knowing that the same afflictions are accomplished in your brethren that are in the world.**
>
> **1 Peter 5:8,9**

Satan goes about seeking whom he may devour. He would love to devour everyone, but he can't. He has to seek people who will allow him to devour them. I don't believe anyone intentionally says, "Yes, I want to be one of the people that Satan ruins." But because of bad decisions, one of which is a decision not to praise God, we give Satan an inroad into our lives. It's just like dropping our guard when we're in a fight. It's allowing Satan to take free punches at us.

Perception or Deception?

We give Satan too much credit. Satan does not have spiritual perception. He can't understand spiritual things, but he is a master of deception. He understands natural things in the carnal realm. He can beat anyone in the natural realm, but when it comes to operating in the spirit realm, he can't compete.

> **Howbeit we speak wisdom among them that are perfect: yet not the wisdom of this world, nor of the princes of this world, that come to nought:**
>
> **But we speak the wisdom of God in a mystery, even the hidden wisdom, which God ordained before the world unto our glory:**
>
> **Which none of the princes of this world knew: for had they known it, they would not have crucified the Lord of glory.**
>
> **1 Corinthians 2:6-8**

If the scribes and Pharisees who were in opposition to the Lord would have had any spiritual perception and wisdom, they would not have crucified the Lord of glory. Jesus prophesied many times that He would die and be resurrected on the third day. He even prophesied the method of His death. If they would have had any spiritual perception, they would have killed Him any other way than on a cross. In fact, they would have done anything except kill Jesus, because He had prophesied His death and His triumph over it.

Satan was the driving force that motivated these people to come against Jesus, and Satan is the one who caused them to crucify Him. If they had operated in any form of spiritual understanding, they would have never crucified Him. Yet Satan went ahead and fulfilled everything God had intended. He played right into the hand of God when he crucified Jesus.

> **But the natural man receiveth not the things of the Spirit of God: for they are foolishness unto him: neither can he know them, because they are spiritually discerned.**
>
> **1 Corinthians 2:14**

A person without the Spirit of God cannot really receive spiritual truth. Satan is without the Spirit of God. Satan is spiritually stupid. Even though the book of Revelation so clearly prophesies the punishment and defeat of Satan, he cannot comprehend it. He cannot believe that what God has said is true; therefore, he'll play right into the hand of the Lord.

The Results of Intercession

Intercession in the Old Testament is very different from intercession in the New Testament. In the Old Testament, the sacrifice hadn't been made yet. In the New Testament, the sacrifice of Jesus Christ has been made. It's a simple matter of taking the victory that has already been purchased and executing it.

I don't believe spiritual warfare has to make a person look beat down, depressed, sad, and discouraged. That's not what spiritual warfare or intercession is all about.

In the Old Testament, there was actually a pleading with God. In Exodus 32:9-12, Moses asked God to repent and not bring His wrath upon the Israelites for making and worshipping the golden calf. There was also a kind of bartering that went on between Abraham and God over the cities of Sodom and Gomorrah. (See Genesis 18:23-33.) Those kinds of things don't work in the New Testament. That is not the type of intercession we are to have.

My little children, of whom I travail in birth again until Christ be formed in you.

Galatians 4:19

Paul speaks of travailing in the spirit, but it has been so blown out of proportion. I believe one of the things that would put the New Testament ministry of intercession and spiritual warfare back in its proper balance is if we started operating in praise. Praise will bind the devil and drive him away quicker than anything else we can do. When an intercessor operates in praise, they are going to focus their attention on the answer instead of the problem. They're going to wind up spending their time with God instead of the devil.

Spending Too Much Time With the Devil

When I got really turned on to the Lord back in 1968 and began casting demons out of people, it was amazing to me that some of the things I had always considered normal weren't so normal — some behaviors actually had demonic spirits behind them. That immediately got my attention, and I started seeing a demon on every doorknob! I remember every time someone had a twitch or a cough, I'd think it must be a demon. I got to where I would spend one to two hours a day binding this spirit, binding that spirit, praying against the devil, and so on.

Now God understood my heart. I believe God is just like a natural father. We see our children go through things that may be out of balance, but that's just part of learning. We don't get upset with them, but correct them and teach them the proper way.

During that period I had some great times with the Lord, but I probably had more demonic problems than I should have — not necessarily something on the inside of me, but Satan attacked me more then than anytime since. I know two or three occasions where I physically fought some demonic forces. I couldn't see them, but they were grabbing me around the throat and choking me. There were times I would wake up from a dream and just be terrified and think, *It was only a dream.* But then I would find myself actually bleeding from something that happened to me.

In 1971, I tried to open a "halfway house" where I could take in addicts to minister to them. I rented a large house which had been a fraternity home, and it was infested with demons. I was there by myself late one night when I was physically attacked by a number of demons. I fought until there was victory, but it was not a pleasant experience!

I know Satan is real. But I am convinced that one of the reasons I was being attacked like that was because I was spending so much time thinking about the devil. I was trying to resist him, but my attention was so much on the devil that I was more aware of Satan's power than I was of God's power.

Finally, the Lord began to bring me out of this. I realized the error of my ways and decided it had to stop. I began to think, *Man, I don't have to spend all my time rebuking and casting down every possible thing that could come against me. If I would just begin to praise God and walk with Him...The best defense is a good offense. If I'm in communion with God, that will automatically stop a lot of the things of the devil.* As I began to implement that into my life, I saw a change in my spiritual warfare.

I still see demons cast out. There are times that the Lord will give me a word of knowledge over someone I am praying for and the demons will come out screaming, kicking, and yelling. But I don't spend hardly any time talking to the devil, because I have learned that praise is strength to still the enemy and the avenger.

As I keep my communion with God, as I worship and praise Him, as I keep my attitude straight and my mind stayed upon the Lord and His Word, the Lord keeps me in perfect peace. That is my immunization against the devil. Since those early years of my walk with the Lord, I am seeing more victories over the devil with less effort. I depend on praise and worship to God as my weapon that stills the enemy, and it's been over twenty years since I have had any manifestation of Satan physically attacking me.

Praise is a powerful weapon. In the midst of all the spiritual warfare teaching, we need to give preeminence to praise. There are a lot of people who would be better off if they spent less time talking to the devil and much more time praising God for Who He is. If they would praise God for the positive, they wouldn't have to spend so much time on the negative.

Satan Knows He Is Defeated

Satan knows his days are numbered, so he is trying his best to thwart the plan of God for people's lives.

Personally, I believe that's the reason Christmas has been compromised as a Christian holiday. Satan has substituted a big, jolly man in a bright red suit for the Lord Jesus. He is trying to draw people away from the true worship of God. However, even with all of its commercialization, Christmas has impacted the secular world to such a degree that during the holidays, I can walk into a department store that normally is playing secular music and hear songs like "Joy to the World" and others that glorify God.

People who don't think about God any other time of the year are bombarded with the Gospel during the Christmas season. I get excited about that, and I realize that Satan can't stand it. He may be successful with a few people, but overall he knows he's already defeated.

Thanksgiving in the United States is one of the most godly holidays we have, because it is a day that was set aside for nothing but thanksgiving and praise towards God for the abundance of things. It is what I call a pure holiday. Yet, it has nearly been passed over with all the other things, such as football games and the after Thanksgiving/pre-Christmas sales. We need to be aware of Satan's devices, which may seem so innocent, and purpose in our hearts and minds to stay in an attitude of praise.

Satan Cannot Stand Praise

Satan was the demonic spiritual power behind the king of Babylon. In chapter 14 of Isaiah, talking about the demise of Satan, he speaks this parable against the king of Babylon.

How hath the oppressor ceased! the golden city ceased!

The Lord hath broken the staff of the wicked, and the sceptre of the rulers.

He who smote the people in wrath with a continual stroke, he that ruled the nations in anger, is persecuted, and none hindereth.

The whole world is at rest, and is quiet: they break forth into singing.

Yea, the fir trees rejoice at thee, and the cedars of Lebanon, saying, Since thou art laid down, no feller is come up against us.

Hell from beneath is moved for thee to meet thee at thy coming: it stirreth up the dead for thee, even all the chief ones of the earth; it hath raised up from their thrones all the kings of the nations.

All they shall speak and say unto thee, Art thou also become weak as we? art thou become like unto us?

Thy pomp is brought down to the grave, and the noise of thy viols: the worm is spread under thee, and the worms cover thee.

How art thou fallen from heaven, O Lucifer, son of the morning! how art thou cut down to the ground, which didst weaken the nations!

For thou hast said in thine heart, I will ascend into heaven, I will exalt my throne above

> the stars of God: I will sit also upon the mount
> of the congregation, in the sides of the north:
>
> I will ascend above the heights of the
> clouds; I will be like the most High.
>
> Isaiah 14:4-14

The only time Satan is called Lucifer in the Bible is in Isaiah 14:12. This scripture clearly gives us the intent of Lucifer's heart when he transgressed and rebelled against God. If we really think about what the motives were in Satan's rebellion, it could totally change our impression about Satan.

Most people think Satan is a total pervert, that he glories in all the things God hates. But Isaiah 14:12-14 shows us just the opposite. Satan actually loved all the things God had — the praise, the worship, the glory, and the honor. Satan's sin was not hating everything God liked; rather, he coveted the things of God. Satan wanted to **be like the most High** (Isaiah 14:14).

Satan's real sin was jealousy of God. Ezekiel 28:14 says he was **the anointed cherub that covereth.** Cherubs are angelic beings who were placed over the mercy seat to protect the holy of holies. (See Exodus 25:19.) So Satan was a created being, an angelic being of God. He was the **anointed cherub that covereth.** That was a high position. Some people speculate that he was an archangel, the position that, according to Jude 9, the angel Michael now holds. That would mean he was in charge of all the other angels, but he wasn't satisfied with that. He wanted the glory, the honor, and the praise that went to God alone. That was his transgression.

I will grant that Satan is the author of all perversion and everything that is anti-God. But I believe the reason he pulls people in that direction is that he's trying to draw them away from God. He is insanely jealous of God, and that gives us a better understanding of why praise to God is strength to still the enemy.

Many people also think Satan was anointed in the area of music. He wanted all the praise, the worship, and the music that was going up to God by the angelic beings for himself. So God overthrew him. But to this day, Satan is driven by jealousy.

What Praise Does to Satan

When we praise and worship God, it reminds Satan of his defeat. Praise to God torments him, so much that he even tried to get Jesus to worship him. When Satan came against Jesus in the wilderness, Jesus was just beginning His ministry. Satan presented Jesus with three temptations, one of which was material gain to try to get Jesus to worship him.

> **Again, the devil taketh him up into an exceeding high mountain, and showeth him all the kingdoms of the world, and the glory of them;**
> **And saith unto him, all these things will I give thee, if thou will fall down and worship me.**
> **Matthew 4:8,9**

Satan does the same thing to us today. He tempts us with material gain to try to get us to worship anything but God.

This goes back to the very heart of what I've said — Satan has always desired the worship that was intended and reserved for God alone. This shows how important the area of praise is to Satan. Satan told Jesus he would give up everything he had in exchange for the praise reserved for God alone. He was and is a fanatic about this! He is totally crazy.

But Satan is not *stupid!* He is an enemy to be reckoned with. We can't take him lightly — he's been at this for thousands of years. However, his extreme jealousy has totally perverted his thinking, and anytime a person begins to praise God, Satan cannot handle it. Satan cannot stand praise to God.

So the next time you find yourself being tempted to sin, being attacked, or facing some problem, lift your voice to heaven and start praising God. I guarantee you that not only will you feel the peace of God come upon you, but you will know the devil is defeated in whatever area you're doing battle. In reality, you are just being a doer of the Word.

Submit yourselves therefore to God. Resist the devil, and he will flee from you.

James 4:7

The Key to Victory

I went to Rome right out of high school, and I remember reading accounts of the Christians who were burned at the stake and thrown to the lions in the Circus Maximus and in the Colosseum in Rome. There are actual reports of emperors who stuck their fingers in their ears and screamed out, "Why do these Christians sing as we kill them?" It was reported that Christians would worship and praise God even in the very last stages of death, and the emperors couldn't handle it. People are afraid of what they can't understand, and I believe the devil has the same reaction. If you want to torment the devil, start praising God. It will drive him away. If you want to confuse the devil, start praising God.

Let the high praises of God be in their mouth, and a twoedged sword in their hand;

To execute vengeance upon the heathen, and punishments upon the people;

To bind their kings with chains, and their nobles with fetters of iron;

To execute upon them the judgment written: this honour have all his saints. Praise ye the Lord.

Psalm 149:6-9

Praise and the Word of God coupled together is how we execute vengeance and judgment upon our enemy, the devil.

These warriors had a two-edged sword in their hand, which is the Word; but they had *high praises* of God on their lips. Together they were a force to be reckoned with. This is available to *all* believers.

Don't wait for your circumstances to change before you praise God. Praising God will make your circumstances change. Your praise terrorizes the enemy. It paralyzes Satan. It neutralizes his power in your life!

Chapter 9

How Praise Affects God

We've looked at how praise affects us and how praise affects Satan, but I believe the way praise affects God is the most important. I know that's kind of a subjective statement, because it depends on where you are. If you're in hand-to-hand combat with the devil, it might be more important for you to learn how praise is strength against the enemy. If you're tormented in your mind and you're struggling with different things, then you might feel that it's more important to know how praise affects the individual. But as far as taking all of these things and listing them according to which is the most important, I believe how praise affects God makes the top of the list.

Ministering to God

Now there were in the church that was at Antioch certain prophets and teachers; as Barnabas, and Simeon that was called Niger, and Lucius of Cyrene, and Manaen, which had been brought up with Herod the tetrarch, and Saul.

**As they ministered to the Lord, and fasted,
the Holy Ghost said, Separate me Barnabas and
Saul for the work whereunto I have called them.**

Acts 13:1,2

Many times we pass over this verse and focus on the results. We talk about how this was the beginning of Paul's ministry and literally hundreds of thousands of people were affected in his lifetime. Then we look to his leadership and at the books he left behind. They comprise about half of the New Testament! Paul affected the world forever.

When the Holy Spirit called Barnabas and Saul, this was a real pivotal time in the history of the Church. But here is an awesome statement we usually don't notice: **As they ministered to the Lord** (Acts 13:2). Now the first time I really read this, that word *ministered* jumped out at me. I just sat back and was amazed. I thought, *How do we minister to the Lord?* I thought that when you minister to someone, you were preaching to them or teaching them. Or it could be that you go and serve a person or do something for them. But how can we minister to the Lord? How are we to serve Him in that way?

I knew one way of ministering to the Lord was by ministering to other people. In Matthew 8:14, we find Peter's mother-in-law with a fever. Jesus went into their house, touched her hand, and the fever left her. Then it says that she **ministered unto them** (v. 15). It's very clear that she did some of the household duties the women of those days would do. She took their coats, washed their feet, fixed food for them, etc. That's a ministry. I'm not minimizing that at all, but it was the only concept of ministry to others I had.

In Acts 13:1,2 it's very clear that these people were fasting and praying and ministering to the Lord. They weren't out serving other people, praying for the sick, or witnessing to the lost. They had come together for the purpose of separating themselves and seeking God. They were there worshipping the Lord. They were glorifying God. As I began to see this, all of a sudden I began to realize that God desires ministry.

Please don't misunderstand me. I'm not saying there is lack or inadequacy with God. God is complete. He is self-contained. If none of us existed, He would still be all-sufficient.

He that loveth not knoweth not God; for God is love.

1 John 4:8

We must look at it through the perspective that God is love. Any person who loves not only has a desire to show that love, but they also have a desire to have love returned unto them. God not only loves us, but He has a need in the sense that He desires us to love Him. That is the way it's supposed to be.

It's not inconceivable that someone who loved us enough to send His Son to this earth to suffer shame and to die for us could also get blessed when we tell Him that we love Him. It's an old religious attitude that tells us we're so unworthy we can't bless God, and the only thing we can do is serve Him as an unworthy slave. Man, that's not so! God changed us. We are now the righteousness of God in Christ, and He desires our love.

To the praise of the glory of his grace, wherein he hath made us accepted in the beloved.

Ephesians 1:6

This is what was behind the creation of man in the first place. Earlier in the book we brought out the point that praise and worship are filling heaven right now. The Bible also says that God has created all things for His pleasure. (See Revelation 4:10,11.) That was the original purpose for creation and is still His purpose for creation today — for His pleasure. Everything was created for His pleasure. But we get so service-oriented thinking, *What does this accomplish? Who is this going to touch?* that many times we forget that if it blesses God, if it ministers unto Him, it doesn't necessarily have to be touching someone else.

An example of this is when I went on vacation with my family in the mountains of Colorado. We like to go where other people don't go. We don't like to go to the big cities. For me, a vacation means getting away and having time with just my family.

We drove as far as our car could drive on this dirt road. Then we got out and walked as far as the trail went, and then we just took out on our own. We were up somewhere around 12,000 feet, and as we came over one of the mountains, we looked down and there was this lake. It was a beautiful lake, with the mountains all around, and beside this lake was a meadow. Now in the mountains there's only a short growing season, but we happened to hit it just perfectly.

We saw some of the most beautiful wild flowers I'd ever seen — some of them four and five feet tall. I had never seen anything like them before, and as I was standing there looking at all of this, I was just amazed. I began to think about God. I thought, *This is amazing! This is awesome! The effort You put into this little spot — all of these flowers.* Man, in all of his great wisdom and technology, couldn't reproduce one of these flowers — even if all the scientists combined their efforts — and there were thousands and thousands of these flowers. The thought also occurred to me that in just a week or so they would all be gone. There was a very good possibility that no one but us would see these flowers, because I didn't know if anyone else had ever been up there.

As I was thinking about all this, I said to Jamie, "Isn't this awesome, that the Lord went to all of this effort? As far as we know, we're the only people who have come this direction and have seen this. God went to all of that effort just for us." And I believe that God would do something like that just for us!

Jamie then quoted Revelation 4:11 to me, **for thy pleasure they are and were created.** She said, "It wouldn't have mattered if anybody would have seen it. *God* got pleasure out of these things that He's made." And all of a sudden, it really began to sink in. This was the same thing the Lord had been showing me — God gets blessed from His creation!

God desires to receive pleasure from the things He created and made. In my mind I thought, *Who did He do this for? There has to be some person this would minister to. There has to be some value to it. God wouldn't put all of this effort into something for no one to see.* But that's wrong thinking, because God got pleasure out of it.

Many times, when it comes to our relationship with the Lord, we do the same thing. We think the only way we can minister unto God is by serving Him through touching other people's lives, by working in a church, witnessing to someone, or praying and interceding on behalf of someone else. Now that does minister unto the Lord, and I am not minimizing that; but I'm saying that there is another area of ministering unto the Lord that most Christians have not seen, and that is that God created us for His pleasure.

Being Intimate With God

God loves us. He wants our praise and worship. Praise ministers unto Him. Praise blesses God. If praise had no other benefit, then that would be reason enough to praise Him. God has given us everything. He literally bankrupted heaven. He took the most precious thing heaven had, which was the Lord Jesus, and sent Him to this earth to redeem us. He did all of these things for us, and God longs and desires for us to praise and worship Him.

I married my wife, Jamie, because I loved her. When I proposed to her, I said, "Jamie, I want you to share the rest of my life with me." I wanted her to share everything with me. Jamie is an excellent wife. She cooks for me and our kids, she cleans the house, she washes the clothes, and she does a lot to take care of our home. She runs a tight ship around our house. She is a perfectionist at organization. She even alphabetizes her spices! But it balances me, because I'm not that way at all.

If anything is misplaced in our house, all I have to do is sit down and think, *Now what is the logical thing to do? Where would this be put if it was put in its proper place?* I think about what Jamie would do in that area and go find it. She is just as predictable as she can be.

We live way up on a mountain, and our shoes get really dirty, so we've got an entryway into the house where she asks us to take our shoes off. I have to be honest and admit I don't always do it, but I appreciate the fact that she is trying to keep our house clean and make it a comfortable place to live. That adds to our marriage!

But if it ever got to a place where she was more concerned about external things than our personal relationship, then those very things she does would cease to minister and be a blessing to me. It would get to where I would hate them. If she yelled, "You take off your shoes or don't come into this house," every time I forgot and was more concerned about the carpet than she was about me, then that would not bless me. It wouldn't minister unto me.

I can go out and hire a cook. I can hire someone to clean my house. If all I wanted was service, I could have done it without getting married. But that's not what marriage is all about. That is not the focus of marriage. You cannot build a marriage based on a clean house, clean dishes, and clean clothes. Marriage is about relationship, and praise God, Jamie is a tremendous blessing to me. Because her first priority is intimacy *with* me, everything else she does *for* me becomes a blessing.

It's the same thing in our relationship with the Lord. Yes, God wants us to serve Him through ministering to other people, through praying for them, and doing good things for other people. But it is not a substitute for our personal relationship with God. I feel that in most cases, Christians don't think they really have anything personal to give God except their service. When most people come to the Lord, they have the attitude, "God, I'm the one in need. You have no need whatsoever." It's a mentality of being totally needy.

We do have needs. We are the ones with all the failures and faults in our life. But it is not totally accurate to see God as having no need, thinking there is nothing we can do for Him except serve. God needs us. He desires us. And we can minister unto Him — not through preaching at Him, not through just doing something for Him, but through loving Him directly. That ministers unto God.

To think that my net worth to God is what I can do for Him or how well I perform is missing what salvation is all about. God isn't just using us as a tool to reach someone else, to reconcile the world to Himself, or to amass great numbers of people following Him. I believe that the Lord would have died for me if I was the only person on the face of the earth. I believe He would have made an atonement for me if I had no one else to minister to and nothing to accomplish for Him. God just loved me and He wants my praise and worship in return.

What God Really Wants From Us

I think some people believe God felt obligated to save us, because He was our Creator and things got so messed up that He had to provide a way out for us. They call that *obligation love.* They quote John 3:16, **God so loved the world,** and when it comes to applying it to their life, they don't see it as a passionate love God has for them. They see it more as pity. And now that their sins are forgiven, the only thing they can do is pay their debt. They've got to go out and serve God, do this and do that, and offer God all of the things they've done. They think that pleases Him.

Of course, I'm not saying it doesn't please God to serve Him, but it doesn't please God if we substitute *things* for *ourselves.* God wants *us.* Praise is giving of ourselves to God — expressing our love and worship to Him. That ministers to God. There are things we can do for the Lord, but there is nothing we can do for Him until we have first given ourselves unto Him. We have given God everything but ourselves. But God wants *us.* He longs for us to love Him. This is really the most important aspect of praise. As we give of ourselves, everything else will fall into place.

Going back to the comparison I gave about my wife and her serving me, that's not the reason I married her. I married her for a relationship. If she got to where she exalted the service and all of those things over me, the very things that now bless me would actually repulse me. That's exactly what God expressed in the Old Testament.

God commanded that sacrifices be offered. He commanded the people to follow Him through all of the solemn feasts, the feast of tabernacles, the day of atonement, and all of the different rituals. Yet, in Isaiah 1 we find that God's people had become rebellious — their hearts had turned away from the Lord and all they had was just a ritual. They had no heart for God. They were just going through the motions, and their hearts were separated from God.

> **"The multitude of your sacrifices — what
> are they to me?" says the Lord. "I have more
> than enough of burnt offerings, of rams and**

> the fat of fattened animals; I have no pleasure
> in the blood of bulls and lambs and goats.
> "When you come to appear before me, who
> has asked this of you, this trampling of my courts?
> "Stop bringing meaningless offerings!"
>
> Isaiah 1:11-13 NIV

Those were things that God commanded. They were right things to do. But the Lord was saying, "I don't want your service. Those were just expressions, pictures, types, and examples of what should be reflected in your heart. If you aren't going to give Me your heart, then away with this other stuff." I believe God could look down at much of our religious observance today and see a similar picture. We have people going to church, paying their tithes, living holy, doing all of these things, yet God is not pleased because He doesn't have their hearts.

God loves you, personally. God longs for you to have personal, intimate communion with Him.

> I will bless the Lord at all times: his praise
> shall continually be in my mouth.
>
> Psalm 34:1

Most people don't know what the word *bless* means when they see it in Scripture. It has become a religious word that we don't really think about. I've heard people say, "Bless the Lord, bless the Lord, bless the Lord," and they think that by repeating those words they are blessing the Lord. Not necessarily.

When the Scripture says *bless the Lord*, it isn't saying to recite those words. Expressing our love and worship to God blesses Him. This is a radical concept to most people, because it doesn't involve any kind of service. We're so *do* oriented, and so *works* oriented, that we feel we must *do* something for God in order to please Him. We've become human *doings* instead of human *beings*.

We hear it preached so much, "Do a work for God! Do something for God! If you aren't doing something, you're worth nothing to God. Your net worth to God is directly proportional to how much you can do." This emphasis leaves an impression in people that God loves them only for what they can do. It reminds me of when you get a milkshake and you stick the straw down in the cup. You suck out everything that's in there and finally, when you get to the end and you hear it go shccccccc, you throw it away. That's the way some of us are. We think, *God, I've ceased to be able to bless people. I'm not doing anything. I know You couldn't love me. There's no point in me existing.*

Many believers have a real sense of obligation to do something for God, but it's all exterior. It's all what they can do *for* God. It's not direct communication with God. I'm trying to elevate this and say that one of the purposes of praise — actually, *the* number one purpose of praise — is to minister unto God. That has to be the priority in every believer's life. Sad to say, it's not the priority. We usually only come to God when we get into trouble, and when we're in trouble, usually the very first thing we quit doing is praising God.

I went through a time like that when I was in Vietnam. I just didn't feel very productive and I thought, *God, there's no point in me living.* I knew that I was still saved and that I'd go to be with the Lord, but I asked the Lord to kill me and take me home because I felt like I was just occupying space. I actually used those exact words. "God, I'm just not benefiting anybody. I have nothing to contribute — there's no point in me existing."

But God gets blessed by our personal love being expressed to Him. We need to recognize that. When my son, Peter, told me, "Dad, you're a good dad," it made me want to get him out of bed, take him horseback riding, and go through the whole day all over again, just so I could hear, "Dad, you're a good dad."

That's the reason we do things for our children — we love them and want to see them blessed. I don't believe God is selfish. I don't believe He gave His Son for us only so we could give back to Him. Man, if there was ever an example of unselfish love, it is God. So I'm not saying that God is only blessing us so He can be blessed in return.

When I give something to my children, I'm giving to bless them because I love them. I don't demand it, but I would love for them to love me in return and to be appreciative. That's part of us. We were made in God's image, and God feels that way. I believe that we have a spirit that was created in His image. There are reflections of God's image in our personality, and the desire that we have to not only give but to receive love is a godly trait. I believe it reflects the heart of God.

If you have had this mentality that all God wanted from you was doing this and doing that, I'm here to tell you that He would like you to just stop awhile every day and praise and worship Him. Spend time with Him the way you would your closest friend — because that's what He wants!

Conclusion

Praise ye the Lord. Praise God in his sanctuary: praise him in the firmament of his power.

Praise him for his mighty acts; praise him according to his excellent greatness.

Praise him with the sound of the trumpet: praise him with the psaltery and harp.

Praise him with the timbrel and dance: praise him with stringed instruments and organs.

Praise him upon the loud cymbals: praise him upon the high sounding cymbals.

Let every thing that hath breath praise the Lord. Praise ye the Lord.

Psalm 150:1-6

God deserves everything we've got! Our goal should be to glorify God the way He deserves to be glorified. Every person reading this book has breath. As long as we have breath, we should be praising God, for if we don't, the very rocks will cry out. (See Luke 19:40.)

When we move into the realm of praise, we move into the heavenly realm. We are operating in the same praise and worship that is going on in heaven at this exact moment.

Make praise a part of your daily life. Keep your mind set on things above. Don't let the cares of this world pull you down, because **if God be for us, who can be against us?** (Romans 8:31). When we praise God, we've got every area covered — we are ministering directly unto God and pleasing Him, we are building ourselves up, we are tormenting the devil, and we are immunizing ourselves against all of the things Satan is bringing against us. That is exciting!

About the Author

Andrew Wommack was brought up in a Christian home in Arlington, Texas, and made a total commitment of his life to the Lord at a very early age. But it was not until he received the baptism of the Holy Spirit as a teenager that he began to experience the power of God in his life.

Since that time, he has served as Pastor of three churches in progressive steps to the ministry God has called him to fulfill: teaching the entire Body of Christ the good news of our New Testament relationship with Jesus Christ.

Andrew is fulfilling this calling as he travels throughout the world sharing the simple truths of God's Word with people of various backgrounds. He is heard on radio stations across America and has distributed over three million cassette tapes of his teachings free of charge.

Books by Andrew Wommack

The Effects of Praise and Worship
Living in the Balance of Grace and Faith
The True Nature of God

To contact Andrew Wommack, write:
Andrew Wommack Ministries
P. O. Box 3333
Colorado Springs, Colorado 80934-3333

In Europe, write:
Andrew Wommack Ministries of Europe
P. O. Box 35
Coventry, CV1 2NE
England

Please include your prayer requests
and comments when you write.

**Copies of this book are available
from your local bookstore.**

Albury Publishing
P. O. Box 470406
Tulsa, Oklahoma 74147-0406

In Canada, contact:
Word Alive
P. O. Box 570
Niverville, Manitoba
Canada ROA 1EO